Nancy Ma

Dancing On Mara Dust:

The True Story Of A South African Farm

Nancy Mathews
Vivien Smith

First published in Great Britain in 2006
By Vivien Clear Publishing
P O Box 95, Darlington, DL1 9BD, England.

A CIP catalogue record for this book is available
from the British Library.
ISBN 10:   0-9552671-0-2
ISBN 13:   978-0-9552671-0-9

The picture of Spitskop Mountain on the front cover is from
an original watercolour by Caroline M. Clear.
The photograph on the back cover is courtesy
of Marietjie Underhay.

Printed and bound in Great Britain by CPI Antony Rowe, Eastbourne

CONTENTS

FOREWORD

This book is the story of my family's struggle for survival in South Africa in the 1920s and 1930s. The place-names are those which were used at that time. As far as possible, conversations have been faithfully reproduced and reflect speech and attitudes of the period.

My grandmother, Harriet Mabel Mathews, who endured many hardships and was latterly crippled with arthritis, was a great formative influence on my life. She died when I was seven years old. I made a promise then that one day I would make sure her story was told to the world. In fact it has been mainly my mother, Nancy Mathews, through writing about her life in South Africa and England, who has produced a remarkable tribute to herself, her parents and her brother, Aubrey. The legacy she leaves is for me, my sister, Hilary, and my children, Caroline and Helen. It has been my privilege to work alongside her in order to bring this story to publication.

I am greatly indebted to Marietjie Underhay of Medike, Limpopo Province, South Africa, for sending me some valuable reference sources and for helping with translation and proof-reading and much more. Thank you, too, to all my ever-helpful and tolerant proof-readers: Caroline and Helen Clear, Francis and Nina Pagan and Hilary Smith, and to Jamie Bradbury for helping a novice in information technology. I am grateful, too, to Alan Wall of Darlington Business Venture and Ed Meikle of Dickinson Dees Solicitors, for their advice. Last but not least, thank you to my husband, Charlie, for being there. Always.

NOTES ON TRANSLATIONS: Every effort has been made to produce accurate translations. My mother was told by those who lived on Dalemain farm that their language, which she spoke fluently, was a dialect of Sesotho. It appears, however, that it is instead a variant of Sepedi. In the 1990s, my mother and uncle were able to make themselves understood, albeit not completely, to speakers of Sepedi living in the Soutpansberg region. Because the language is that of eighty years ago, and because everyone mentioned in the book has either died or left the area, it has been impossible to provide exact spellings of certain words or phrases. Where I was unable to obtain exact spelling, I have taken the liberty of attempting to reproduce the wonderful sound of these words. To my mother is due credit for remembering the wonderful cadences of this language, after a span of some eighty years. All mistakes or discrepancies in translation and in editing are therefore mine, all credit for remembering the spoken words, hers.

Vivien Smith   September 2006

GLOSSARY

Baas/basie	Boss, young boss	Mosese	Cloth covering the buttocks
Bechuanaland	Botswana	Mozambique	Maputo
Biltong	Dried, salted meat	Naartjies	Tangerines
		Naboomspruit	Mookgopong
Boerewors	Sausage	Northern Transvaal	Limpopo Province
Bok-duwweltjies	A type of thorn-bush	Nyasaland	Malawi
Braaivleis	Barbecue	Opskud musiek	Fast dance music
Brinjals	Aubergines		
Dassies	Rock rabbits	Panga	Hunting knife
Dollos	Witchdoctor's knuckle-bones	Pietersburg	Polokwane
		Piet-my-vrou	Redchested cuckoo
Dumela	Greetings		
Flying ants	Termites; alates	Potgietersrus	Mogalakwena
Go-away bird	Grey lourie	Potjiepot	Alcoholic stew; potjiekos
Heidelburg	Lesedi		
Hout River	Mogwadi River	Pretoria	Tshwane
Johannesburg	Gauteng	Pronking	Playful leaping of buck
Kgosi	King, chief		
Knobkerrie	Stout stick with knob at end	Rondavel	A round hut
		Sand River	Polokwani River
Koffie en beskuit	Coffee and rusks	Sorghum	Millet
Koppie	Hill	Southn. Rhodesia	Zimbabwe
Kraal	Enclosure	Spook	Ghost
Krantz	Ravine	Stoep (stoop)	Verandah
Ladysmith	Emnambithi-Ladysmith	Tannie, Tante	Aunt(ie)
		Theto	Cloth covering the genitalia
Leguaan	Monitor lizard		
Louis Trichardt	Makhado	Totsiens	Goodbye
Mieliemeel	Polenta	Tshetsha!	Hurry!
Mielies	Maize	Uldulela	Goodbye
Morogo	Wild spinach	Vastrap	A type of polka

MAP OF THE TREK - 1925

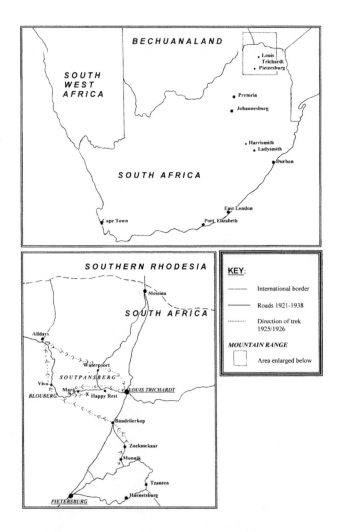

CHAPTER 1
PRESTON,
ENGLAND. 1941

It was war-time: we were in the icy grip of winter. The snow, which had fallen for several days, had stopped and now it was freezing hard. Only a few months ago I had started my nursing career and this was my first experience of night duty.

The spine-chilling wail of the air-raid siren cut the night air. This was followed by the hospital's loudspeaker which bellowed repeatedly, "Operation Air Raid Shelter – all personnel on duty immediately, please!"

Nurse Mathews. Inset: Sister Smith.

The staff had been trained in the correct procedures to follow in the event of an air raid and now we wasted no time in getting to our posts and executing our duties with speed and efficiency. Along the corridors hurried doctors, sisters, nurses and porters, all pushing trolleys and wheelchairs carrying patients down several floors to the safety of the hospital's air raid shelter. The sisters and staff nurses quickly collected as many boxes of pills, bottles of medicine and first aid kits as they could carry for the patients on the wards as well as for any other casualties they might encounter.

The senior sister walked down the ward towards me and said in a quiet voice, "Now, Nurse Mathews, you'll have to be left alone in the ward with those two patients behind the curtains at the far end. They're both very old and much too ill to be

11

moved, so you'll have to sit with them till the air raid is over. Call me on the emergency phone if anything happens and, well, good luck." With that she trundled the last patient in a wheelchair out of the ward towards the lift. I heard the ward doors close with a click.

I listened to the lift's clanking as it hurtled down to the basement. I felt too afraid to move; I stood in the blacked-out ward and stared at the sinister corners where the curtains had been drawn around the unconscious patients. My only source of light was a small torch which the sister had dropped into the pocket of my uniform as she hurried out of the ward.

When the muffled shouting of instructions from the doctors, nurses and porters, the moans and groans of the patients, the rattling of the trolleys, creaking of the wheelchairs and the clanging of the lifts had all died away, everything became very quiet.

One hour later, I was still standing alone and afraid in the centre of this long ward of fifty beds in Preston Royal Infirmary in Lancashire when I became aware of a droning noise, first soft, then increasingly louder, overhead. I realised it must be the RAF Spitfires roaring into combat. After a while the noise died away and all was quiet again.

The town hall clock struck twelve. I shuddered and wondered what I was most afraid of: a direct hit from a German bomb? Those two old and terminally ill patients whose lives were ebbing away behind the curtains in two corners of the ward? Or the ghostly Grey Lady who was said to walk silently through the wards at midnight?

Eventually my eyes grew accustomed to the darkness and I felt bold enough to tiptoe to the window to wish those gallant young airmen good luck, courage and a safe return home. Through a small hole in the blackout curtain, I watched the planes pass overhead till they melted into the starry sky.

It was a crisply cold and clear night. The moon was riding high and shone white; the stars were polished silver against the velvet sky. I looked out across the rooftops of rows of terrace houses in one of the most densely-populated areas of Preston. Chimneys were casting dark, slanting shadows on the snow-capped roofs which were glistening in the moonlight.   Once all the planes had passed by, the world seemed eerily serene.

I began to feel a very great longing to be back home. Tears welled up in my eyes and trickled down my cheeks as memories came crowding down the years – memories of my happy childhood and the home in the Transvaal bush which I had left behind. I was transported over land and sea to South Africa, thousands of miles away. Forgotten were the bombs, the ghostly Grey Lady and the two old patients behind curtains at the end of the ward. I was home again, surrounded by everyone I had known and loved. There was our farm, Dalemain, still safely nestling in the arms of our mountain, patiently awaiting our return. Everything was peaceful and quiet, bathed in the glow of the yellow African moon. Nothing seemed to have changed. My mother and father were sitting chatting on the stoep about the day's happenings on the farm while my mother fanned away the mosquitoes and my father puffed away at his pipe.

Fireflies darted and flitted to and fro in confused patterns. My brother, Aubrey, and I were playing hide and seek with our friends and our dog, Crusoe. Our shrieks of excitement echoed up the mountain to the troops of baboons, who barked back in anger and frustration at being so rudely disturbed.

I heard the yaps and chilling screams of the jackals out on their nightly hunt for food, the owls' hooting far away over the flat veld, and the cicadas' high-pitched zithering in the warm, balmy night air. How wonderful it was to be safe and happy again, deep in the heart of the bushveld.

I was so lost in my reverie that I did not hear the ward door open, nor did I hear any approaching footsteps till I was very sharply jerked back into reality by the angry voice of Matron.

"*What are* you doing at the window, nurse? Block that hole up at once and come away from it. Don't you know there's a war on?"

"Yes, Miss Hindle, I'm sorry – I just forgot for a moment."

"You *forgot?*"

Her sarcasm silenced me. I blinked back the tears – it would be useless to explain to her as I knew that she wouldn't understand, so I meekly and very guiltily followed her down the ward to the drawn curtains.

I was fervently hoping and praying that those two lives had not ended during my brief escape to the far Northern Transvaal.

CHAPTER 2
THE BEGINNING OF THE JOURNEY

Canon Mathews

My father, Stuart, was the eldest son of Canon William Mathews who lived with his wife and family of nine in the precincts of several churches, including Carlisle Cathedral and, at the turn of the twentieth century, Bassingham Entire parish near Lincoln. The Canon was an Oxford University graduate, tall and well built with a bushy, grey beard which grew almost to his waist: a typical Victorian gentleman. He had well-defined ambitions for his children – medicine, law or ministry in the church for his sons; well-connected marriages for his daughters. He was a disciplinarian and his parishioners always treated him with great respect and courtesy. His wife, on the other hand, was a gentle, kind lady who was very popular with rich and poor alike. All four daughters followed in their mother's footsteps by attending Girton College for Ladies. Two of them married well while the others lived at the vicarage under the patronage of their father. However Kate, the eldest daughter, was strong-minded and, against her father's wishes, trained as a nurse. During the First World War she became the matron of a field hospital in France. After the war ended she was awarded the Royal Red Cross for her untiring devotion to nursing services on the front line.

Four of the Canon's sons became doctors, but Stuart was a very adventurous boy and could not settle down to a quiet professional life. It was hoped that, as the eldest son, Stuart would be ordained in the Anglican Church and to this end he was sent to Rossall School in Fleetwood, Lancashire, where it was expected he would complete his schooling before entering Oxford University.

Rossall School was not far away from the busy seaport of Fleetwood. Stuart often used to go down to the docks and watch the tall ships. He loved to listen to the sound of the water's slopping against the quayside, the ropes' creaking against bollards, the smell of tar, smoke and spices; he liked to watch the swaying of the mastheads and gaze at the ever-beckoning horizon. Above all, he enjoyed the bustle of people from places far and near, the promise of new lands, new faces, new adventures. The sailors were used to seeing him and often came to chat to him and to spin him yarns about far away places. Stuart became friendly with some of the sailors and in 1882, at the age of 15, he eventually persuaded one of the older men to smuggle him aboard a ship that was bound for the South China seas.

The day of his departure dawned wet and windy. Stuart went to a secret meeting place behind some old, disused wine casks and waited for what must have seemed hours. After a while, the unmistakable smell of the old sailor's tobacco wafted towards him. Quickly he climbed onto the man's back. To camouflage the large lump on his back, the sailor threw his sou'wester over them both and walked up the gangplank. The rest of the crew were too engrossed in their work or in merry-making below to notice anything unusual. Once on board, Stuart hid behind some packing chests in the stores. He was in high spirits – the old sailor had found him some comfortable blankets, food and drink, a tin of biscuits, half a bottle of beer and there was a conveniently placed tap with drinking water close by. He was suddenly experiencing freedom, and the thrill of this adventure remained with him all his life.

A couple of days out to sea, his old sailor friend fell and broke his ankle. Stuart was discovered and marched up to the Captain's office where he was severely reprimanded. As the ship was too far out to sea to turn round, Stuart was peremptorily transferred to a homebound ship where he was put to work scrubbing the decks until the ship docked in Fleetwood harbour. He was handed over to the Headmaster of Rossall School and to his father, who were both waiting for him on the quayside. Stuart was taken back to school, given a beating by the Head and punished by his father, as well. He did not set sail again for many years, but neither the spirit of adventure and wanderlust, nor the same defiance of authority that his sister Kate had also shown in choosing nursing against her father's wishes, ever left him.

To all outward appearances, though, Stuart settled

down. He completed his schooling at Rossall and attended an agricultural college in Cornwall where he gained considerable knowledge of farming and of general management. After college he worked as a farm manager in England and Canada, and as a cowboy on a ranch in America.

At the age of thirty-one, he married Lucy Slater who was born in Carlisle and who was to bear him five children. Years later he confided to my mother that his marriage to Lucy had not been happy. Whether this was due to incompatibility or to the strain on the relationship caused by his wanderlust is unclear since soon afterwards, Stuart and Lucy sailed to South Africa where they remained until Stuart enlisted in the Border Regiment during the Boer War. According to the 1901 census, Lucy and two children, Frederick, who died at a young age, and John (Herbert), born in South Africa, were living at the Lincolnshire rectory, together with the Canon and two of his daughters. In 1903, Lucy rejoined Stuart in South Africa and bore him two further children, Molly and Norman, before returning to England where their youngest son, Robin, was born. At the outbreak of the First World War, Stuart re-enlisted in the army. As Second Lieutenant, he was wounded in the chest and side with shrapnel while fighting in France and returned to

Stuart Mathews 1914

England. In May of 1918, Lucy died of tuberculosis; a small tombstone in Dacre churchyard marks her grave.

* * * * *

My mother, Mabel Woodhead, was the eighth of nine children. She was born in Stainton, a small village near Penrith in the heart of the Lake District, in 1882, the year Stuart ran away to sea. Mabel's father, Seth, a graduate of Cambridge University, was headmaster of Stainton School where for forty-six years, he taught all the village children. He was a tall, thin man with a long, divided grey beard and for years was known, like Canon Mathews, to be very strict and a firm upholder of Victorian values. His wife, Mary Allinson, was the daughter of a local farmer.

Mabel and her brothers and sisters had to attend church twice every Sunday, either in the village school, or more usually at Dacre church, three miles away. Evenings were spent singing round the family's piano or organ in the parlour. The children were not allowed to do any courting before they turned eighteen and even then they had to

Mabel Woodhead 1914

obey a seven o'clock curfew. It is hardly surprising that only four of the nine married, as any suitor had indeed to be of a very determined disposition.

Mabel is listed in the 1901 census as a seamstress. Later she was appointed as assistant teacher at Stainton School. Here she remained till the outbreak of the First World War, when she went to Edinburgh to train as a nurse and eventually took up a post as nursing sister at Warwick Square Nursing Home, where Stuart was admitted, suffering from shrapnel wounds, after he had been invalided out of the army. Mabel was thirty-six years old and Stuart fifty-one. My father used to tell everybody that his meeting with Mabel was love at first sight. They married in 1919, three months after they met. Neither the Woodheads nor the Mathewses approved of the match, because of the age difference between Stuart and Mabel, and because it was only a few months since Lucy's death. Besides, Stuart's son, John Herbert, was now twenty years old; the younger children, Molly, Norman and Robin, were still at school. My parents married hundreds of miles away from both families, on the south coast of England in the home town of one of his army friends, Ronnie Cheales. Ronnie Cheales was a rebellious individual who had also, in the face of family disapproval, eloped with the daughter of a Jamaican family. Winnie Cheales was Mabel's matron-of-honour, and Stuart's best man was an ex-army officer who was also a cousin of the King of Belgium.

* * * * *

Stuart had received several letters from an army colleague, Colonel Bridgeman, who tried to persuade him to return to South Africa to manage a farm there. Mabel was naturally concerned: she didn't want to go to a wild, unknown country and leave her close-knit, comfortable family, her friends and the Cumberland with its rolling green hills, lakes and fells that she loved. However, Stuart's charm and his powers of persuasion prevailed and Mabel eventually agreed to travel to South Africa, on the understanding that should she not like it or should she become homesick, then they would return to England. Arrangements had to be made for Stuart's children: it was decided that while Herbert was to continue working in England, Molly, Norman and Robin would be left in the care of Lucy's family, the Slaters at Wetheral, so that they could complete their education in England.

Canon Mathews was heard to say that if his wayward eldest son did decide to return to South Africa, he would be disinherited. No further communication between father and son took place after this, and the Canon died shortly afterwards.

Stuart and Mabel, who was not to see her parents, nor many of her brothers and sisters again, sailed from Southampton on the Edinburgh Castle on a wet, cold, foggy winter's day. After an uneventful but pleasant voyage of several weeks, they disembarked in Cape Town and transferred to the Cape-to-Cairo northbound train for a five-day journey to Pietersburg, where they had arranged to be met by Colonel Bridgeman.

Mabel enjoyed the first leg of the train journey through the spectacular blue Cape mountains. As the train chugged north through the Cape Province, across the thousand-mile stretch of the flat, arid Karoo desert, she began to suffer from heat exhaustion, which worsened as the train puffed laboriously through the Orange Free State where wind blew continuously across the bare veld.

They crossed into the Transvaal where the bushveld became wilder, with thick thorn-bushes growing right up to the railway tracks. Dust devils spiralled across the flats. Heat-waves shimmered and danced off the railway sleepers and the continuous shrill of cicadas was almost deafening.

At last the train drew into the quiet little town of Pietersburg, where Colonel Bridgeman was waiting for them. Colonel Bridgeman ordered the servants to load their luggage onto the two-horse buggy then he took my parents to the best hotel in town for a meal. Unfortunately the waiter brought the wrong dish to the Colonel, which incensed him.

"Do you know who I am?" he asked the unhappy waiter. "I am Colonel The Honourable Bridgeman and don't you forget it!" Mabel was shocked to hear someone being spoken to so arrogantly. She felt very uncomfortable and ate the rest of her meal in silence. After coffee, Colonel Bridgeman escorted them back to the buggy and helped them on board, took the reins and the buggy set off at a brisk pace. It trundled over the rust-coloured, narrow and dusty track through dense bush and scrub on the last forty miles of their journey from England.

As they drove along they watched scores of wild animals leaping across the road in front of them and across the bushveld. Mabel had previously seen only hand-drawn pictures of wild animals. Snakes slithered across the road and in the dry grass and twisted round branches that overhung the road. Monkeys and baboons startled her when they tried to jump up onto the roof of the buggy, which made the horses snort and rear, cutting the air with their hooves.

They passed several groups of scantily clad women, some carrying very large earthenware pots of water on their heads and others, large bundles of firewood. Several of the women had a baby tied securely onto their backs with goat or buckskins. Mabel, who had taught geography to the village children of Stainton, was fascinated.

After a few hours the buggy passed between two lines of large blue-gum trees bordering some well-tended gardens, then through a gate before it finally drew up at Munnik farm house, their new home.

The farm was stocked with dairy cows, beef cattle, pigs, goats, fat-tailed sheep, donkeys, two horses, several dogs and cats, the latter being a legacy left by former occupants. The house itself was a large, square brick building with a bright red corrugated iron roof which also spanned a wide verandah. As Munnik lay in the malaria zone, all the doors and windows were protected from mosquitoes by wire netting. The house had three bedrooms, a parlour and a dining-room which opened out onto the back verandah, with an adjacent kitchen, all of which were sparsely furnished. A second dining-room led out onto the front verandah, which like the back one, was used only on special occasions.

Not long after we arrived at Munnik, a feral cat chose part of the back verandah as a home for herself and her kittens. This area was declared out of bounds to Aubrey and me. The rest of the verandah was partitioned off and used as our bathroom. Along one wall was a four foot zinc bath with handles at each end, and a makeshift wash-stand on which stood a large wash bowl and jug, brightly painted with flowers.

As there was no running water in the house, water was collected each day from a well nearby and poured into a tank which stood outside the back door. Some of this water was heated on the kitchen stove and then carried in buckets through the verandah and dining-room into the bathroom. Dirty bath water was carried outside and poured into another tank which was used to water the vegetable garden in the dry season. There was no electricity, so we used candles and paraffin lamps every evening. Our lavatory comprised a little tin hut hidden in a clump of bushes and was reached by climbing over a stile about fifty yards away from the back door.

Each morning the lavatory was Sannitized by sprinkling lime powder down through the home-made wooden box seat, into the hole. This system appeared to work very well.

Aubrey was born in Pietersburg hospital ten months after my parents arrived at Munnik and I was born eighteen months later at Haenertsburg. My father hired a nurse called Eileen to look after my mother. Both my parents described her as a lovely young girl, kind and happy. During my birth, my father busied himself with grooming his big black thoroughbred mare called Nancy. When he was called in to see me for the first time, he apparently said, "What a beautiful little girl. I'm going to call her Nancy after my beautiful mare." Nancy is what I have always been known as by the family, even though I was christened Caroline (after my aunts and my father's mother), Mabel (after my mother) and Eileen (after my nurse). I often used to feel that life had not been kind to me and that, having been named after a beautiful nurse and a beautiful horse, I should also have been a raving beauty.

Mabel, Aubrey, Nancy
1922

My father used to ride round the farm every morning on horseback to inspect the livestock and the land which was planted with mielies and sorghum and to look for any damage caused by ostriches, to the barbed wire fences which bordered the lands. He often used to sit me on the front of his saddle and take me with him on these inspections. I loved riding around the veld as there was so much to see: colourful birds, newly born calves, donkeys and kids and wild buck.

* * * * *

The farm had no tractor; instead a one-share plough drawn by four oxen, tilled the land. Rain fell regularly, the land was fertile and the crops grew well. At the end of the season a threshing machine which had been ordered months earlier, arrived. Soon the corn and mielies were being thrashed out and shovelled into one-hundred-pound sacks which would be taken to Munnik station by ox wagon then loaded onto the train for transporting to Pietersburg market. At the side of the house in the storeroom, we kept some of the sacks of grain which everyone on the farm was free to use. A corn-grinder ground the mielies into a coarse meal from which we made porridge.

* * * * *

When Aubrey was just two years old, he wandered off through the gate at the end of the garden while my mother was busy in the kitchen. Suddenly she realized he was nowhere to be found. My father searched everywhere and called him repeatedly but there was no response. Then, looking through his binoculars, he spotted a tiny figure about a quarter of a mile away amongst a group of cattle across the veld. The big, brown and white Hereford bull with his curly head sniffed at Aubrey's heels as he toddled through the short grass. The rest of the herd followed this unusual twosome.

My father jumped onto his horse and galloped towards Aubrey who continued to wander away from the house. When he reached Aubrey, my father jumped off his horse, scooped up Aubrey then climbed back on the horse and cantered back home with him. When Aubrey was asked where he was going, he said, "See mummy." After that incident, the gate was locked.

Several years later, my mother told us that at about this time she had miscarried twins, a boy and a girl, after she was thrown from a horse when she and my father rode over to visit some neighbours. Aubrey and I were much too young to have known anything about it, and I felt very disappointed when she told us because we would both have loved another brother and sister to play with.

After our midday dinner we all used to lie down in our bedrooms for a nap during the hottest part of the afternoon. Aubrey and I would then get up and go out to play while my father sat reading in the parlour. My mother always washed and put on a freshly laundered dress for afternoon tea at four o'clock, when the servant came to announce that tea was ready. Teapot, milk jug, sugar basin, four cups and saucers were laid on a tray on the table and next to that, a plate of buns, scones, jam and cream.

* * * * *

One day my father noticed an advertisement in the paper from a young college student who wanted to have some practical experience of farming. As my father was in need of some

Photo taken by Eric Rennie 1924.
Nancy was suffering from tummy-ache.

help on the farm, he wrote to invite the student to work on the farm.

Eric Rennie was about twenty years old. My father showed him over the farm and taught him about sheep and cattle-dipping, branding, treating livestock for various diseases, about ploughing and reaping and how to use the threshing machine. They complemented each other well, the charismatic middle-aged English war veteran and the idealistic if slightly unpractical young agricultural student.

24

One day my father gave Eric a saw and asked him to climb up a tree to cut off an overhanging branch. My father stood back and watched him. Eric shinned up the tree trunk, manoeuvred himself along the branch a few feet, and sitting straddle-legged across the branch about ten feet off the ground, he started to saw vigorously at the branch between him and the tree trunk. My father stood with his arms akimbo, Aubrey and I beside him, and watched Eric sawing away energetically. A slow smile spread across my father's face and he said, "Just look at that silly ass!" With that the branch gave way and it and Eric came crashing to the ground. My father was very amused at this and said, "Eric, you silly ass, you should have been sitting at the trunk end of the tree, not at the end of the branch."

Eric emerged from the branch and leaves a bit scratched and bruised, but otherwise none the worse, and said he'd know next time, but they hadn't taught him that at college! He stayed with us for the summer holidays. My father liked him and asked Eric to accompany us on our trek to find a new farm in the Transvaal, but Eric's mother was not keen on the idea so Eric returned to Johannesburg Agricultural College a wiser young man, having gained the practical experience of farming he needed.

* * * * *

At the side of the house and surrounded by wire netting was a hen run in which we kept a number of turkeys and hens. At night time the turkeys were shut into their hut and the hens roosted in the three big thorn trees where they were safe from the marauding jackals and the leguaans that waddled around looking for eggs outside the run.

We had two self-appointed nannies, Sanni and Makivella, aged about eleven and twelve, who lived on our farm. Sanni decided to look after Aubrey and Makivella chose to look after me. Their clothing comprised a small string which connected a little red cloth at the front (a "theto") with a small, triangular piece of buckskin at the back ("mosese"). A few wire bracelets adorned their ankles and some beads were tied round their necks. Their hair was always cut short and shaved into a circle on top.

One summer's morning they took us to the tall blue-gum trees that lined the driveway, and spread out blankets in the shade where we all sat and played. After a while, I began to feel very sleepy, so I lay down on the rug. Makivella picked a long, grass stalk and began to chew the sweet end then as I lay there she started to sing a gentle little African lullaby. The doves high up in the trees were calling "Oct-tober", "Oct-tober" over and over again, and I drifted off to sleep.

Some time later I woke up. I opened my eyes and gazed up at the long, slender, stiff green leaves of the blue-gums as they swayed and rattled, making curious patterns against the deep blue background of the African summer sky. I heard Makivella giggle softly. I turned my head towards her. She was still chewing the grass stalk. When she saw I was awake, she began to laugh louder and pointed to the hen run.

I looked round and saw Aubrey frantically trying to catch a big turkey cock that was running up and down against the wire net fencing in an attempt at losing its pursuer. Aubrey, however, was determined to catch it. Eventually after a number of attempts, he succeeded in putting his arm round its neck, brought it to a halt, scrambled onto its back and tucked his bare feet under its wings.

The turkey sped off round the hen run with Aubrey firmly seated on its back. He was laughing and calling to me to "come and have a ride" but the turkey looked so big, and I really did not like the look of its purple head and wattles, or the loud gobble-gobble made by the other turkeys.

A few minutes later, the turkey found a small gap in the wire fencing, and bent low and crawled through. Aubrey was scraped off its back and left on the inside of the fence, while the turkey, still gobbling and protesting loudly, ran off with ungainly strides into the bush. Aubrey stood up, covered in feathers and dust, just as my father came out onto the verandah and demanded to know why so much noise was coming from the hen run. We shook our heads in wide-eyed innocence. Since it had been such good fun, we couldn't spoil our turkey trot by telling our father about it.

There were a number of black families living on Munnik farm. Throughout the week they worked very hard, but reserved Saturday nights for celebrating. They used to fill several big earthenware pots with a very potent beer which they brewed from sorghum. We could clearly hear the noise, the singing, shouting and the throbbing drumbeat. Often fights broke out, which tragically occasionally resulted in someone's death.

One Sunday morning a young girl, clearly very upset, came running up to the house. She was crying loudly that some men were going to bury her mother alive. My father saddled his horse and galloped to the place that the girl had described, near a local village. He was just in time to see a group of men lowering a body wrapped in blankets into a very shallow grave. My father jumped off his horse and told them to lift the body up and lay it by the side of the grave. They did this very unwillingly; my father knelt down and unwrapped the top half of the body. He saw that the woman was not dead, though her breathing was very shallow and she was motionless. She smelt very strongly of beer. He felt her pulse which was very faint. My father told them she was not dead, just very drunk.

Most of the mourners ran away terrified, thinking that she had had a spell cast on her by the witchdoctor and that she was now an evil spirit. My father made some of the men carry her back to her hut. When she eventually recovered, the villagers were really frightened of her and would not allow her to live amongst them for fear that her evil spirit would bewitch them. A few days after her burial, she and her daughter packed up their blankets and left the district for good.

* * * * *

Every year my father was required to appear before a medical board in Pietersburg for assessment for his medical pension, which amounted to the princely sum of thirty-six pounds per annum. One dark morning we all set off very early on a journey from Munnik to Pietersburg for my father's check-up. It was very dark and we had to travel along a narrow track cut through the bush. Two carthorses were inspanned and hitched to the buggy. At the head of the buggy was a container on a pole from which swung a paraffin lamp which threw a faint light over the rough, sandy road.

27

Thick bush grew right down to the roadside. The track was narrow and the strip of grass growing in the centre brushed the undercarriage of the buggy. The horses trotted along slowly. My father and mother sat on the front seat and Aubrey and I sat in the back. As we travelled along I peered into the dense, dark bush. Suddenly I became aware of some very strange black and white animals running alongside the buggy. I could see only that they were about the size of baboons, with very big eyes, though I could not tell whether they were baboons, large monkeys or cats. Their eyes kept staring at us as we moved through the inky black night. I was frightened of them and became mesmerised by them. I wanted my mother and father to look but they were so busy trying to keep the buggy safely on the road that I decided not to distract them. Many years later I mentioned this incident to Aubrey and he said that he had seen them, too, but only on his side of the buggy. Had we both been imagining the same thing? As dawn began to break these creatures seemed to slow down and then disappear into the bush. I can not remember seeing them again because when we drove back the next morning it was still dark and Aubrey and I slept throughout the long journey, almost till we got to Munnik.

CHAPTER 3
SOME FAMOUS NAMES

I was three years old. One morning my mother called us inside and said, "We're having some visitors to spend the day with us today, so I want you both to be good." She washed our faces and hands, put our best clothes on and told us to go and play on the verandah.

Delicious smells wafted through the kitchen window. We peeped round the door to see what was happening. My mother and the cook were both very busy: the cook was preparing meat and vegetables and my mother was baking scones and fairy cakes. For a while we watched with interest but we soon became bored and went outside to look out for the visitors.

A little later, a horse-drawn buggy driven by an elderly man drew up alongside the house and he and his wife climbed out. My father went outside immediately to greet them and shook hands warmly, then went indoors for coffee. The cook brought out some fresh orange juice and scones to Aubrey and me.

The sound of laughter and chattering drifted outside. We jumped up and down, trying to look through the window surreptitiously to see the visitors, until at last we heard the door open. My mother came out to us and said, "I want you both to come in and meet our guests."

We went into the lounge to see an old (everyone is old when you're not quite four) lady sitting in a rocking chair quietly rocking to and fro. She was short and plump, with dark, silvering hair raked back and secured with tortoiseshell combs on each side of her head and caught up into a big bun at the back, firmly kept in place with hairpins. When she saw us, she looked up and smiled, then hugged and kissed us both.

"Aubrey, Nancy – say hello to General and Mrs Smuts," said my father. I bit my lip and stared. Aubrey nudged me, and we chanted in unison, "Hello General and Mrs Smuts."

As the leader of the South African party, which my father supported, General Smuts occasionally addressed party meetings at Munnik. My father always attended these political gatherings as he said General Smuts was a "good man". The opposition, the National Party, was known to be anti-English and considered General Smuts to be a traitor to the Boer cause.

General Smuts came towards us with his hands outstretched and scooped me up into his arms. He had grey hair and was slender, dressed in a grey suit with a starched white collar. He sat down on his chair, placed me on his knee and said, "I love little girls," and kissed me on my forehead and cheek. I didn't feel comfortable or very happy. I didn't like his neatly trimmed little white pointed beard and I hoped he wasn't going to insist on kissing me again. I slowly wriggled and squirmed off his knee, then stood staring at him from a little way off. He smiled and asked, "Don't you want to kiss Oom Jan?" I shook my head, although I really didn't mean to be rude to him. However, he didn't appear to be upset. He stood up, smiled and patted my head and Aubrey's, then put his hand into his pocket, brought out two small packets of sweets and gave us one each.

We thanked him and then ran outside and gave Sanni and Makivella some of the sweets. Sweets were a very special treat as we were only ever given them for birthdays or at Christmas. However, after we had shared them out, we became engrossed in a game of tiggy and soon forgot about our visitors.

I was still feeling guilty about not wanting to sit on his knee, when General Smuts came outside and started talking to us. He played five-stones and hide-and-seek with us until my father came out and invited him in for lunch. By now I had warmed to him because I had won most of the games. Aubrey and I had our lunch on the verandah while the grown-ups ate in the dining-room. After lunch we were sent to our bedroom to have our afternoon nap.

When we woke up, we found that my new friend and his wife had left, after thanking my parents for a very pleasant day. Although I liked him, secretly I was really very relieved, as I dreaded having to kiss him and his beard goodbye.

Of course we were much too young to know what an important visitor we had had and that I had refused to kiss an internationally-respected political leader who played such a key part in the development of the Union of South Africa. I wonder how many other people can claim to have manipulated this clever political player into knowingly being on the losing side.

My mother used to order books from Johannesburg and some even from England. She used to read these to Aubrey and me: classics such as Robinson Crusoe, Peter Rabbit and Alice in Wonderland, as well as tales about witches and wizards, fairies, animals and adventure stories. The stories that we enjoyed the most were about kings and queens, handsome princes and beautiful princesses in sparkling gowns and jewels. I would imagine that I was a princess in a flowing pink and gold gown and that Aubrey was a prince in a brightly-coloured, braided suit with an ermine-edged cloak.

It was the end of May, 1925. My mother had just finished reading us a story about a king, queen and princess in a far-off land. She closed the book and told us she had a surprise for us. Prince Edward, she said, the son of the present King and Queen of England, would be passing through Munnik station on his way to Johannesburg on Friday morning and we would all be going there to wave to him.

"Isn't that wonderful news?" she said. We were so excited that we jumped up and down several times. Never in our wildest dreams could we have thought such a thing could happen to us: that we would see a real, live Prince, the sort we'd read about in the books from England. Two days was a very long time to wait, so we tried to ease the tension as best we could by running round to all the farmhands to tell them the news. Very few of them had any idea who we were talking about, as they'd never heard of our royal family, but they listened to us patiently. We ran home and collected as many picture books as we could find about kings, queens and princes, all in their purple and gold ceremonial robes and wearing diamond, ruby and emerald crowns, and then showed everybody examples of what the Prince of Wales, due into Munnik station on Friday, would look like.

When they saw the pictures showing the swirling purple, gold and red cloaks and crowns with glittering jewels, they became very interested and began to share our excitement. Important occasions were celebrated by their chiefs and kings in ceremonial dress. This normally consisted of horns, colourful feathers, beads and porcupine quills round their heads and braided into their hair, a leopard skin slung over the shoulders and jackal tails hanging down from their waists.

My mother was kept busy all the next day pressing my father's dark suit and polishing all his medals. She took out of the wardrobe her favourite dress and ironed it, ready for the following morning.

Early that Friday a group of about ten men, fifteen women and thirty children gathered at the back of the house where they were all given tea, thick chunks of bread and jam and a handful of my mother's home-made butterscotch toffee. It was midsummer. Already at nine in the morning the sun was riding high. My father remarked that this day was going to be a scorcher.

The buggy was brought round to the front of the house. The two horses had been well groomed, and their harnesses were jingling and shining in the sun. Aubrey and I had been scrubbed from top to toe and were dressed in our only decent set of clothes. My mother herself looked like a princess in a pretty lavender dress and a large picture hat, and with a sunshade matching her dress. My father, in his dark suit and with his war medals shining across his chest, could himself have passed as a real prince. Very excited, we danced round him then the four of us climbed up into the buggy and started off on the journey to the railway station. The farmhands and their families were also very excited. They laughed and talked loudly, danced and sang as they walked behind the buggy all the way to the station. They even made up a song to celebrate the occasion, all about "The Great White Son of the Great White King."

They had decided to celebrate the arrival of the Great White Son in an appropriately colourful fashion. The men had stuck turkey tail feathers and porcupine quills into their hair. One paraded smartly in my mother's discarded picture hat and sunshade and one even tried to hobble painfully along in a pair of pink and white high-heeled shoes which, apart from being totally unsuitable, were far too small. The women wore bright-coloured material or towels round their waists, with red, yellow, blue and white beads round their foreheads, necks, upper arms and wrists. Round their ankles were several strands of copper wire and dried seedpods which clinked and rattled as they walked. The boys were barefoot and wore loin clothes made of rabbit skin; the girls wore beads round their waists above their theto and mosese. They were noisily sucking the butterscotch toffee that my mother had given them.

We soon arrived at the little station, where we climbed down from the buggy and went to stand close to the railway lines. The station consisted of two little tin sheds: the stationmaster's office and a small storeroom. A big water tank that towered above the railway line was connected by a thick black rubber pipe to a tap which was used to fill up the steam engines with water on their thirsty journeys to and from Southern Rhodesia.

We stood waiting patiently; it was now mid-morning. Aubrey and I chased one another round and round my mother, till we were told to behave as we were creasing her dress. We began to play with the other children, who were just as excited as we were. However, as time went by we became tired and irritable and to add to our misery, the ground was burning our bare feet. Hoping to find some shade, we went to stand close to my mother, but by now the sun was directly overhead so there was practically no shade at all.

The Station Master, a short, thick-set middle-aged Afrikaans man with thinning grey hair and a neat moustache, could not tell us how long we would have to wait. Although it was out of his control, he apologised because the train was so late and invited my parents, Aubrey and me, into his office for a drink. Aubrey and I asked for orange juice, which was nearly the same temperature as the tea given to my parents. We went back onto the platform, since it was stifling hot inside the little tin office. We stood waiting and hoping that the train would soon arrive. The farmhands and their wives and families had been offered neither water, orange juice nor tea and the babies on their mothers' backs were crying loudly. The Station Master eventually found some mugs and jars and told them that they could find drinking water at the back of the hut.

Time passed: I was bored and was becoming irritable. I glanced at my mother. Her peaches-and-cream complexion had now become red and blotchy. My father peeled off his jacket with the shining medals because he said he "felt like a cooked lobster".

33

Aubrey started whining and asking when the Prince was coming. I'd suffered more than enough and began to cry. We were all very tired; there was little shade and nowhere to sit.

I whimpered, "Let's go home." My mother, too, was ready to go, saying, "Yes, we'd better go, Stuart, we've all been standing in this boiling heat for nearly three hours." My father nodded and said, "I'll wait till half past one, and if he doesn't make an appearance by then, well, I'll have to tell these poor blighters not to wait any longer." We were all by now limp and dejected and had lost all interest in the Prince.

About ten minutes later we heard a shout of, "Mulilo!" (Fire). We turned our heads and looked to our left and sure enough there was a puff of smoke in the distance. Everyone rose to their feet and once again started talking and laughing. Aubrey and I immediately felt much better, and didn't notice that we were now hopping from one foot to the other. My mother tried desperately to cool her burning red face by flicking her Olde English Lavender-scented lace hanky. My father put on his jacket again, his medals jingling as he struggled to pull the sleeves over his damp shirt, muttering, "About time he showed up – he's at least three hours late!"

Slowly the large, black steam engine, whistling continually and loudly as it approached, came round the corner into view. I became so excited with each passing second that I could hardly breathe. Aubrey and I jumped up and down and clapped our hands. The tension was almost unbearable. At last we were going to see a real, live Prince, wearing a crown of gold, diamonds and rubies! I thought it a pity that neither the King nor the Queen was going to be there.

We lined up close to the railway tracks so that we could see the train better. The huge engine slowed down as it came into view, then puffing, wheezing and belching steam, it passed slowly by, followed by coal trucks and other carriages. So far we'd seen only the engine driver, his face blackened with coal, smiling and waving to us.

We were desperately looking down the line of carriages trying to find our Prince; we scanned each approaching window keenly. The train screeched and clanked to a near halt. Then my father shouted, "There he is – wave your flags!" whereupon he

34

and my mother began to wave their Union Jacks. I looked hard at the train but I couldn't see anybody to wave at. Then both my father and mother pointed to a thin little man with a very red face and neck. He was dressed in a khaki bush helmet and open-necked bush shirt and leaned out of an open window as he smoked a cigarette. I asked, "Where's the Prince?" My mother pointed to the thin little man in khaki. "That's him – wave to him, he'll be right beside us in a minute."

I was so tired and so very disappointed to see just an ordinary, thin little man in a khaki shirt, and with a bush helmet on his head instead of the glittering crown I'd imagined, that I burst out crying and was wailing loudly when the train slowly passed by us, with the Prince of Wales leaning out of the window and smiling. He was so close that he couldn't help but hear me. He looked down at me and started to laugh, then flicked the butt end of his cigarette towards me, shouting as he passed, "Sorry I can't stop!" The glowing cigarette end fell right onto my bare foot. The Prince looked at me, laughed and shouted, "Sorry, little girl!"

I had been bitterly disappointed about his appearance, but now I positively hated the little man who had made me wait so long and then burned my foot. I vowed never to listen to another story about a prince again. My mother and father laughed when Aubrey said, "He looked funny, didn't he? Just - ordinary."

The rest of the entourage said nothing. I'm sure they must have quite justifiably wondered what all the fuss had been about because he was not dressed any differently from the boers they were so used to seeing.

The train gathered speed as the last coach passed us and we all stood watching it chug round the bend and out of sight. I was only too pleased to see the back of it.

We climbed into the buggy. I was disappointed and sobbing as I could still feel the sting of the cigarette butt on my foot. We were thankful to get home and out of the searing heat of the midday sun. The farmhands and their families behind the buggy were all quite subdued as they trudged back home up the little hill. They were neither singing nor dancing; we heard just a muffled murmur of voices and the occasional click of disbelief.

35

Next day my father asked our two housemaids what they thought of the King of England's son. They shook their heads and said, "Hau! Baas, I dunno, he not like we think. He not like our chiefs and kings – they always dress very smart in their beads and skins."

Both my mother and father agreed that they would have been much more impressed had the Prince of Wales been dressed in leopard skins, claws, teeth, beads and jackals' tails. I, of course, agreed and decided I couldn't and wouldn't ever forgive him for looking so ordinary and for throwing his cigarette onto my foot.

Wagon & Donkeys.

CHAPTER 4
TREKKING

Although my father enjoyed working on the farm at Munnik and had built up a good working relationship with Colonel Bridgeman, he had always dreamed about owning his own farm and working his own land. He had made several enquiries about available plots but there were no farms for sale anywhere near Munnik. He was not, however, a person to be easily deterred. After Aubrey and I had been put to bed, my parents used to stay up late into the night and discuss plans for the future. They had heard that land was more easily available in the northern Transvaal, and had come to the conclusion that they would have to leave Munnik and the security of paid employment and trek northwards in search of land to farm. My mother told Aubrey and me that we would soon be leaving our home and travelling about in a covered wagon to a place many miles away.

This sounded very exciting: we wanted to take Sanni and Makivella and all our dogs and cats with us, but my mother said that would be impossible because space on the wagon was restricted. She did, however, allow us to choose one dog to travel with us: we chose Bonzo, a lively and sturdily-built mongrel with a short brown-and-white coat. My father took his favourite horse, Nancy.

At that time there was no form of public transport to isolated regions in the bushveld, so long distances had to be travelled either on horseback, in donkey carts or in ox-wagons. A few weeks after the decision to trek had been made, a covered wagon drawn by sixteen donkeys trundled up the drive and drew to a halt in front of the verandah. My father came out and spoke to the young driver; together they unharnessed the donkeys and took them down into the mielie lands where they left them to graze for a few days.

My mother and father busied themselves with packing up the belongings that we were going to take on the long trek ahead of us. My mother and the cook baked pies, rusks, bread and biscuits which they packed into wooden boxes, as well as mieliemeel and other dried provisions that we would need on the journey. My father busied himself making the inside of the wagon as habitable and comfortable as he could. He put down mattresses, made up beds and arranged the food boxes along the sides of the wagon.

We found good homes for all the pets and left some cats and dogs with the new farm manager. David, one of the farmhands, volunteered to come with us as our driver and general help. My father was very pleased; he liked and respected David and thought him a very sensible and reliable man.

At last it was time for our departure. We all woke at the crack of dawn and ate a good breakfast. Aubrey and I then ran out to watch the inspanning of the donkeys. The two leading donkeys had both bridle and reins; the other fourteen wore halters which connected them to the main central chain of the wagon.

Once my father and David had made a last-minute inspection of each donkey and the wagon, we were ready to leave. My father lifted Aubrey and me onto the wagon then helped my mother up. David climbed onto the front seat, took up the reins and cracked his long whip. A young boy guided the lead donkey down the driveway and onto the road; the ragged line of donkeys straightened out as they took the strain, then the boy stood back and waved, shouting, "Goodoo bye", and we waved and shouted back till the farm was out of sight.

Once on the road the donkeys broke into a trot; my father followed on Nancy, and Bonzo ran behind the wagon. We had begun our journey into the unknown. Whatever fears and worries my parents may have had, of course, Aubrey and I did not know. To us, aged four and five, it was a great adventure and we crawled and rolled round and played on the mattresses on the floor of our new moving home.

The wagon was very long; there was plenty of room for Aubrey and me to run up and down. The wooden crates along the sides also served as seats and a double mattress and two single ones were laid out towards the front. One or two pieces of furniture were stacked at the back of the wagon. Strong tarpaulin which covered the frame, kept out the sunlight and provided protection against wild animals. Nancy followed, tethered to the back of the wagon. After we had travelled a few miles, the donkeys' initial enthusiasm waned and they slowed down from a trot to a leisurely walk. As the sun climbed higher, their pace became an unenthusiastic plod.

We were heading in a north westerly direction towards the great Soutpansberg mountain range in the far Northern Transvaal. The few roads that existed in those early pioneering days of the 1920s were sandy, dusty tracks, which quickly deteriorated into mudslides after a heavy rain.

I lay down on my mattress and drifted off to sleep, listening to the wagon wheels as their steel bands ground over the sand and grit on the tracks. When I woke up we had stopped and outspanned near a little river. Some of the donkeys were standing and drinking in the river, others were grazing quietly on the opposite bank. My mother and David were busy preparing the meal; the kettle, perched on a tripod over a bright little fire, was singing merrily. We placed our folding picnic chairs round the fire and ate a pork pie and salad, washed down with a mug of tea made with condensed milk.

My father unsaddled Nancy and let her and the donkeys rest in the shade of a thorn-bush. After a few hours, we inspanned the team again, washed the plates and cutlery and stacked them away in the wagon. David and my father stamped out the fire and covered the ashes with soil, then we were on our way once more. Just before sunset, we chose a convenient place close to a stream, where we would camp. Nancy and the donkeys were turned loose to graze before they were tethered to the wagon for the night. David gathered grass and sticks and soon a fire was burning. My mother prepared meat, vegetables and potatoes and made a stew in the black three-legged stew-pot which was balanced over the bright, crackling fire. After supper my mother took us down to the river where she bathed us then put us to bed in the wagon. The inky blackness of the vast, barren veld was broken only by the light from our little fire. I lay listening to the frogs' croaking till I fell asleep.

Next morning at daybreak we had a hearty breakfast and washed in the river. My mother, Aubrey and I packed away the stewpot, plates and cutlery and filled our drinking bags with fresh water. My father and David inspanned the donkeys and saddled up Nancy. Once more we stamped out the fire, covered the embers with soil and climbed into the wagon. This was to be our daily routine for the next six months.

I often wonder if my mother, who was by now forty-three years old and who had so very recently left her home, family and friends in the English Lake District, would ever have consented to go out to South Africa, let alone been persuaded to trek round the wild, lonely bushveld with her husband and two young children in such primitive transport, had she realized what lay before her.

She was a quiet, serene north-country woman with a very direct gaze and the tendency to speak bluntly. She had implicit faith in my father's judgement and hardly ever questioned his decisions, no matter what the circumstances. He, on the other hand, had a devilish sense of humour, a thirst for adventure and great self-confidence. My parents complemented each other perfectly and hardly a cross word passed between them.

We travelled on slowly towards the Soutpansberg range which beckoned in the hazy blue distance. The area south of the Soutpansberg was very flat and dry; small umbrella-thorn-bushes were often the only vegetation. They had very sharp, hooked thorns and it was difficult to untangle anything that was caught up on them.

Periodically we would see a lonely little farmhouse set back in the bush. My father would sometimes ride up to the house to make enquiries about farms for sale. On occasion he came back saying that although there were people living there he was not able to communicate with them because they were Afrikaans and neither party understood the other's language. At other times he came cantering back to the wagon to say that we had been invited to spend a few days there. We were very grateful for this hospitality and always accepted their invitations.

These houses were built of brick with galvanized tin roofs, and were whitewashed inside and out. The floors were made of red mud or cement and were polished to a high sheen every day to make them look and feel like glass. The families were usually very happy and united families and often had several children. Their lifestyle was simple and quiet. The menfolk tended the livestock and worked on the land all day, ploughing with a team of oxen and reaping in season. The women occupied themselves in the house where they sewed, knitted, cooked and baked bread and rusks. They invariably made their homes very comfortable and kept everything clean and pretty. Every evening, the family sat down together and the head of the household said grace before each meal and read a passage from the family Bible, which was often the only book in the house. Their kitchen shelves were lined with rows of bottled fruit, chutney, marmalade and jam made from their fruit trees. A large pantry at the coolest end of the house housed home-cured bacon sides and hams, eggs, biltong and roasted coffee beans.

Life in the wagon after a while became monotonous, so Aubrey and I welcomed these stops. We invariably had several playmates who would very happily share their home-made rag dolls, carved wooden animals and clay building blocks. A rope

41

swing occasionally hung from a tree and sometimes a monkey with a strap round its waist was tied to a pole in the middle of the yard, though I was uncertain about the reason for this cruelly enforced captivity. The fact that we could not speak each other's language was no barrier to a group of lively children and we played and laughed together all day long.

While David was entertained by the servants who worked on these farms, my father and mother enjoyed the company of the farmer and his wife. They often sat up late, talking about farming, politics and travel. At ten o'clock in the morning we would be called in to have "koffie en beskuit" with the grown-ups. The coffee was always delicious, made in a hand-sewn muslin bag in a tall coffee-pot. Boiling water was poured on to ground coffee and the pot was then placed on the stove to simmer. Beskuit, a long, sweet rusk made of bread, was so hard that we had to dunk it in our coffee in order to be able to bite into it, but we loved it. I have to agree with my parents: I have never tasted better coffee than this.

These farmers were very friendly people and their hospitality to weary travellers was overwhelming. They would never accept payment of any kind, and assured us over and over again how much they had enjoyed our company and how sad they were to see us leave. One family in particular I remember were the Van der Walts, who lived on a farm on the slopes of the Soutpansberg mountain range. Mr Van der Walt allowed big game hunting on his farm, and their sitting-room and verandah walls were completely covered with the skins of leopard, lion, monkey, baboon and snake, as well as the horns of bushbuck, waterbuck and kudu. Over their floors were spread the pelts of lion, leopard and cheetah, whose heads and mouths were open to reveal some vicious teeth. I was very frightened of them. We stayed with the Van der Walts for several days, and left rested and revived. Just before we left we all loaded the wagon with fruit which Mrs Van der Walt had either bottled or canned, as well as packs of rusks and biltong, bread, home-cured hams, sides of bacon and a two-gallon can full of freshly-squeezed orange juice.

Finally David said goodbye to his new-found friends. My father and Mr Van der Walt shook hands, my mother, Aubrey and I kissed the family, then we all climbed into the wagon.

David cracked his whip, the donkeys led by a young boy who lived on the Van der Walts' farm, took the strain and we were on our way again. The wagon jolted forwards; we waved and shouted. Heat-waves shimmered and danced on the little tin roof. We felt sad as we watched the house and the family melt into the heat haze as we drove away. We knew we would never see these people again.

We continued on our journey northwards and westwards, along the foothills of the Soutpansberg mountain range. At midday we stopped for a short break; when the sun began to dip towards the horizon, we camped by the roadside. The weather grew hotter and hotter. My father climbed off Nancy and sat beside David in the shade at the front of the wagon; Nancy and Bonzo both kept close to the back of the wagon which shielded them from the burning rays of the sun, while the donkeys plodded slowly along the dusty little track. The land to our left was brown, flat and dry and stretched across to the hazy, blue horizon which appeared to be moving in shimmering heat-waves. Small tufts of brown grass and thorn-bushes grew in patches on the red, bare, windswept earth and marula trees close to the road offered a few moments of shade when the donkeys and the wagon passed slowly underneath.

Baboons and monkeys scampered back and forth across the road or sat at the roadside and stared inquisitively as we drove by. Occasionally a brave young male would try to climb up onto the front or back of the wagon; my father sometimes had to fire a shot into the air to frighten him off, in case he got inside the wagon where we were sitting. The gunshot sent the troop scampering into the bush for cover, only to reappear shortly afterwards and continue to torment us.

We saw several herds of springbok and gazed in wonderment as they crossed the road in graceful high leaps and disappeared into the bush. Sometimes we disturbed wild pigs as they grubbed and rooted at the roadside. They ran off, grunting and squealing, with their tails straight up in the air. Flocks of pheasants, guinea-fowl and partridge ran and flapped noisily into the shelter of the bush and brilliant red, yellow, blue and green butterflies flitted about in their hundreds.

43

Sometimes we stopped close to a group of mud huts, which was a sure sign that there would be a river, dam or spring nearby for our animals. David always enjoyed making enquiries at the huts for fresh water for our canvas drinking bags as well as for Nancy and the donkeys. Often when he returned he was followed by a few young women covered in their traditional red cloth and buckskin edged with beads. Each woman carried an enormous clay pot on her head and chattered and laughed as she walked gracefully towards us with the strings of brightly-coloured beads clicking and jingling round her forehead, neck, wrists and ankles.

On one occasion when a group of women approached the wagon, they lifted the pots off their heads and onto the ground, smiled and greeted him with, "Dumela Kgosi!!" then sat quietly down behind the pots. David said, "They bring presents for you." One pot contained water, one sour milk, one mieliemeel porridge, one meat and wild spinach, while one was full of a very potent thick, brown porridgey beer. We ate as much of the food as we could. My father had a cup of the beer, while David had three cups, then poured the rest into a gallon milk can to take on the journey.

The girls sat watching us. They giggled shyly, obviously pleased that we'd enjoyed their food. To have refused their hospitality would have been a grave insult. My father thanked them and gave them each a bag of salt and a bag of sugar. They were very pleased with this, as they were many miles from any trading store. At the end of the meal, the girls stood up, lifted the pots onto their heads, smiled shyly and said, "Uldumela" (farewell), then they all walked away as they had come, in single file back home, still laughing and talking loudly.

Some time later we approached the end of the Soutpansberg range; a few miles further on we found ourselves near a large, flat saltpan with large pyramids of glistening, white salt which had recently been mined and was waiting to be transported by covered ox-wagon to Pietersburg. At the far end of the saltpan we noticed a little tin hut. My father jumped off Nancy and went over to introduce himself.

When he returned, he told us that the Mine Manager, a Mr Glesotti, had invited us all to his house on a hill overlooking the saltpans. My father led the wagon up the road to the house.

44

Mr Glesotti was a South African-born bachelor of Italian descent. He had very black hair and an imposing moustache. He was middle-aged, not very tall, plump and deeply sun-tanned. He spoke with a slight Italian accent. He lived with one manservant who had assumed the role of butler and also cooked for him as though he were a king. Every evening this servant laid Mr Glesotti's dinner table immaculately with a dazzling white damask tablecloth and napkins and sparkling silver cutlery and bone china dishes.

At eight o'clock precisely we all went into the dining-room. Mr Glesotti was in full evening dress with a bow tie. When my father remarked that it was unusual to find someone in evening dress in such a desolate area, Mr Glesotti said, "I've always changed for dinner. It keeps up the standard, you know, even though I very seldom have company; I'm much too far off the beaten track for visitors."

The next day we said goodbye to Mr Glesotti but before we left he said to my father, "You know, Mr Mathews, I don't think you should go any further west: you're getting very close to lion country and it would be very dangerous for you all and your donkeys." My father said he had planned to trek further afield and that he still had a little way to travel. He and Mr Glesotti shook hands, and Mr Glesotti wished us well. We watched him wave goodbye till he vanished into the white glare of the saltpan.

One evening my father announced that he was going out into the veld to shoot a couple of guinea-fowl for the pot. While he was away, a bush policeman in full uniform rode up on horseback. Very few policemen patrolled this vast area and it was indeed unusual to meet one in the midst of the backveld. The constable stopped when he came up to the wagon, jumped off his horse and introduced himself to my mother. He was Afrikaans and could barely speak English, but he managed to tell my mother that he was hoping to reach before nightfall, an isolated farmhouse still a very long way off in the opposite direction to that in which we were travelling. My mother made him a cup of tea and invited him to wait till my father returned from shooting something for the pot.

Soon my father arrived, carrying a large peacock in a bag over his shoulder. My mother introduced him to the policeman and after hearing that he was hoping to reach the little farmhouse before dark, my father said, "You won't arrive there for many hours: would you like to have some supper with us and then bed down underneath the wagon for the night, and tomorrow after an early breakfast you can be on your way?" The policeman was very grateful and they sat talking in the moonlight while the peacock stew inside the charred pot on the tripod bubbled away.

When the stew was ready we all sat round the little camp table and enjoyed a very tasty meal. The policeman, with his mouth full of peacock, said, "Mrs Mefyous, what a wonderful meal. What kind of meat is it? It tastes like guinea-fowl, but much nicer and more tender."

My mother looked at my father, who began to laugh and said, "Well now, if I tell you that, you'll arrest us because you've just eaten a peacock – a protected royal game bird."

The policeman seemed quite taken aback, but then he began to laugh and said, "Well, Mr Mefyous, how could I arrest anyone who has given me such a friendly welcome and a particularly wonderful meal – after all I did eat with you! But," he added seriously, "you must burn the evidence – the feathers."

He told us that about ten miles further along there was an isolated little up-country store, which my mother and father were very pleased to hear. He said it was set back, well off the little dirt road we were travelling on, and we would have to keep a sharp eye in order to spot it because it was very small. He wrapped one of our blankets round himself and spent the night with David under the wagon. He left early the next morning on his long, lonely beat over the bushveld.

One blistering afternoon, after a few days' driving through the hard-baked land, we spotted the glint of a tin roof in the distance and made a detour towards it. There we found the little store the policeman had told us about. It was run by a middle-aged German couple, Mr and Mrs Moeschell, who were very friendly and invited us to outspan and spend the night with them. Their little store was like an oasis in the desert, especially to the locals who lived in these isolated, sun-baked flatlands. We were treated to a meal of wild boar, and then Aubrey and I were put to bed inside the house while the Moeschells chatted to my parents on the verandah. David spent the night in a mud hut belonging to one of the Moeschells' shop assistants.

Next morning my mother and father stocked up with tinned vegetables and soup, mieliemeel, water and tinned fruit, and plenty of oranges, pawpaws, pineapples and peaches. The Moeschells gave Aubrey and me each a bag of sweets and nuts which we chewed and crunched noisily. These old shopkeepers were very popular with the locals who had to walk many miles every week to buy food such as mieliemeel and sorghum (their staple diet), salt, beans and blankets. We sometimes saw groups of women walking in single file with huge sacks of grain balanced on their heads while carrying goatskin bags containing salt and beans in one hand and a rolled-up blanket in the other. Often peacefully sleeping babies were tied onto their backs and covered with another goatskin. They trudged along the little track, all singing in harmony under the relentless rays of the sun.

The floor of the Moeschells' house was different from that of the other houses we had visited. Instead of having red polished cement, or being draped with the pelts of wild animals, the floors were covered completely with cork. Mr Moeschell explained to my father that polished cement was too slippery and cold, and animal skins attracted white ants and beetles, but cork imported from Portugal had the advantage of maintaining a constant temperature, it felt pleasant underfoot and it could not be eaten by ants.

The following morning we inspanned the donkeys, hugged the Moeschells and wished them well and drove away from them and their lonely little store.

We journeyed on for a few more days, getting very close to the Blouberg Mountain, so named because from a distance it shone a deep blue, in the far North Western Transvaal. On our journey through the bushveld we had travelled through sparsely populated country, sometimes for days, before we had seen either a farm or a village of mud huts, but in this remote and desolate area, between Alldays and Platjan on the border of Bechuanaland, there was no sign of any human habitation. It was a place of pitiless heat. The sun rose in the morning at four thirty

47

and travelled across a cloudless blue sky to end in a blaze of brilliant orange in the west.

One night we camped near a stream very close to the foothills of the Blouberg Mountain. I heard my mother ask my father to turn back as she was beginning to feel very uneasy. My father promised he would think about it after he'd been out to shoot for the pot, and he and David went off into the bush.

The donkeys were feeding on the hay we had brought for them, and we kept quite close to the wagon. Aubrey and I were playing with Bonzo while my mother gathered sticks nearby to kindle a fire for our evening meal. All of a sudden she started to run towards us and said urgently, "Quick! Get into the wagon!" She pushed us up and lifted Bonzo into the wagon too, then hurriedly climbed up after us. We wanted to know what the matter was. She said, "I think I can hear lions roaring." We all sat listening intently. Sure enough, we could hear them in the distance. Aubrey and I started to cry, and Bonzo began to growl. My mother told us to be quiet. She shouted for my father but the veld was so flat that her voice was deadened. There was no answer from my father or David.

The donkeys grew restless and turned to look in one direction. My mother fastened the canvas flaps of the wagon and we sat very still inside the wagon. Through the openings we could just see the yellow African moon rising across the flats and we heard the nightjar's melancholy call, "Good Lord, deliverrrr us!" The roars of the lions seemed to be ever nearer and we sat frozen with fear. After what seemed to be an eternity, we heard some bushes' snapping close by. Our eyes flicked round the wagon as we tried to locate the source of the noise. Aubrey whispered loudly, "What's that?" My mother put her finger to her lips. "Shhh!" Bonzo started to growl again and we held his mouth tight shut. My mother whispered, "Lord save us!" and held Aubrey and me tight against her. We heard a scratching on the canvas flaps at the back of the wagon, then my father's cheerful voice saying, "Hello, anybody home?"

We all cried with relief to see him again. We told him about the lions, but as he and David had set off in another direction, they had heard nothing. Nevertheless they built a big fire beside the donkeys and kept a four-hourly watch beside it throughout the night. The donkeys huddled close together.

Next morning David went out for a walk and returned with news of a lone travelling Jewish trader a mile away who had had many of his donkeys killed or badly mauled by lions the previous evening. After hearing this, my mother refused to go any further and my father agreed that it would really be foolish to continue, but he said we would have to stay there that night as the donkeys and his horse needed to be rested before we started back. He shot a guinea-fowl for our evening meal and a rabbit for Bonzo. We collected as many branches as we could find and piled them in a heap, ready for the night watch but fortunately we did not hear the lions again.

The next morning before we left, my father, Aubrey and I went to look for Bonzo. He had not answered our calls and must have wandered off during the night. Whistling and calling repeatedly, we walked up towards Blouberg Mountain. We listened to our voices echoing up the krantzes, but still Bonzo did not appear. Several vultures further up the mountain were perching on trees, and some of them were squabbling raucously on the ground under the branches.

My father said, "Come on – we'd better get back to the wagon or your mother will be getting anxious." We turned round and walked back, still hoping Bonzo would come bounding out of the bush, but my father, having seen the vultures, secretly feared the worst.

The brown veld, repeatedly scoured by dry, baking winds, stretched bleakly to the horizon. Travelling eastwards, along the northern foothills of the Soutpansberg, we came across a mound of stones overgrown with yellow tufts of dry grass. A little wooden cross rotted by the weather and badly eaten by ants had fallen over and lay on its side. We wondered who else could have wandered so deep into this forsaken part of the country. My father bent down and straightened the crumbling little cross and secured it with stones, then we walked away, leaving the little grave in the lonely veld. David had inspanned the donkeys by the time we returned and my mother had packed away everything in the wagon. As we drove off, Aubrey and I kept calling and looking back for Bonzo, but we never saw him again.

49

We headed northeast and trekked along the northern slopes of the Soutpansberg. Wildlife was plentiful and we saw many kinds of buck, baboons, monkeys, hyenas, wild pig, porcupine and a variety of brilliantly plumed birds. Occasionally the wagon wheels ran over snakes which were left wriggling on the road behind us.

Sometimes we stopped at farms overnight; sometimes we camped and rested at the side of the road. We all felt much happier at having left lion country behind us. This region was just as arid as the Blouberg region though we now passed several gigantic baobab trees. David climbed up some of the bigger ones and picked the fruit growing at the end of their branches. He cracked the hard, melon-shaped shell, took out the pips and gave them to us to suck. They were very tart but also very refreshing. My father told us that the Voortrekker women had also used them to brew a thirst-quenching drink, as well as a yeast substitute in bread. We often picked up brilliantly coloured stones along the road – unpolished jewels of crimson, emerald, turquoise, blue and gold.

After several more weeks of travelling and stopping, we saw a little tin-roofed house standing off the road, and a windmill close by. We were running short of water so my father decided to go down to the house to ask for help. A tall man with an upright, military bearing in a wide bush hat came out. As he approached, my father cried in astonishment, "Well, bless my soul! It's Ronnie Cheales!"

The two men grasped each other's arms for several minutes. They were both very surprised to meet an old acquaintance in the midst of such desolation, in a place where there was little vegetation, just hard, red, sun-baked earth as far as the eye could see.

Ronnie Cheales had passed out of Sandhurst Military Academy and had also been an Oxford don. At the beginning of the Great War, he had been sent to fight in France where he and my father had met, and where Ronnie Cheales had been awarded several medals for bravery. He was a very forceful character: shortly after receiving these medals, he had been discharged from the army for insubordination to a superior officer. My father had not heard from him since my parents' wedding, where Ronnie Cheales had been my father's best man.

After resting with the Cheales family for a few days, we decided to travel over the mountain towards the southern side of the Soutpansberg range, because the northern side was almost totally uninhabited and desolate. The narrow, steep little road up the mountain was so muddy from continual mountain mists that the donkeys, straining in their harness, slipped and slid and my father and David had great difficulty in keeping the wagon on the road. Rocks and cliffs towered on our right, while on our left there was a sheer drop of hundreds of feet into a deep ravine.

We spent a full day in navigating the pass, but it was worth it: the view that met us as we reached the top of the mountain was breathtaking. The veld sprawled away on either side below us. The barren flatlands shimmered away to the horizon then faded into the sky.

The road down the mountain was very steep and stony. David led the donkeys and my father at the back of the wagon applied or slackened the brakes until we were very relieved to eventually reach the bottom of the pass.

We decided to make our way along the foothills of the Soutpansberg towards Louis Trichardt.

Mabel beside post box

CHAPTER 5
MARA

In 1835 Louis Trichardt, along with other Voortrekker leaders, decided to leave the Cape Province and head north in an attempt to find land free from the shackles of the British fiscal system. For the next few years their covered ox-wagons, which provided homes to their wives and families and shelter for their livestock, trundled over flatlands and mountain ranges and through swollen rivers. After some months' travelling, however, disagreements arose among the Voortrekker leaders and they eventually decided to follow separate routes. In 1836 Louis Trichardt's party camped in the Soutpansberg area before continuing on its journey to Delagoa Bay. The group survived numerous attacks by some of the local people and was, as well, decimated by an outbreak of malaria. Only a few survivors, mostly very ill, eventually reached Mozambique.

Meanwhile, other settlers arrived in the Soutpansberg; the settlement grew and in 1898 when the Zuid Afrikaansche Republiek gained control of the area, the town was named Louis Trichardt. In the 1920s it was still a small town that nestled in the foothills of the Soutpansberg and boasted a school, a doctor, a dentist, a lawyer, a barber-cum-hairdresser's shop, a courthouse, and Zway's General Stores which sold practically everything from hardware and clothing to farming equipment. One long, straight main street stretched down a hill from north to south. Near the top of the hill, the large courthouse faced several small, colourful little shops, each with a verandah opening out onto the street. At the bottom of the main road on one side stood Louis Trichardt High School and the General Hospital, close to the railway station. Leading off the main street was a side street of little shanty shops, where everything from pins and needles to blankets, sacks of corn and cheap clothing, was for sale. A woman's dress cost eighteen pence, a man's jacket two shillings and sixpence and a full suit could cost up to a pound. Goods for sale were supplied from convoys of ox wagons which had journeyed northwards from the Cape Province, Durban, Johannesburg or Pretoria.

These dusty little shops bustled with customers and bulged with goods stacked precariously from the floorboards right up to the ceiling. Some of the fastest-selling articles appeared to be the colourful silk saris bought by the small Asian community, and the brightly-coloured beads which the African women bought to make bracelets, necklaces, head-dresses and to decorate their clothes.

There were two churches in Louis Trichardt. One was the Church of England, a small red-brick church at the end of one of the side streets, while the other was the large, imposing Dutch Reformed church which dominated the town from the main street on the brow of the hill. Its walls were built of a cream-coloured brick and the roof was red-tiled. A very high steeple was topped with a golden weathercock, which swung merrily round in the wind. Every Sunday and on religious festivals the bell rang out to call the faithful to church, and Afrikaners would come from far and wide in ox wagons, donkey or mule carts or on horseback to worship. They filled their church to capacity. They were constantly reminded of the sacrifices of their ancestors by the cemetery opposite, where so many of the Voortrekkers from the Cape had been laid to rest.

For some of the families, attending church involved a two-day journey to Louis Trichardt and a two-day journey home, so they loaded their wagons and carts with provisions. They loved their church and were very devout Christians: their God was a merciless authoritarian who demanded and received strict observance.

We spent a few days resting on the outskirts of Louis Trichardt before we bought food and provisions for the next stage of our journey. We inspanned the donkeys who had by now rested well and had all remained remarkably healthy, strong and fat throughout the long, hard trek. We continued westwards along the foothills of the Soutpansberg, where the road was sandy and stony and the wagon bumped along uncomfortably.

A few miles outside the town, the road snaked along a long, steep hill with a rocky precipice on one side. The donkeys strained at the harness and chains. We all jumped off the wagon and tried to help by pushing it but halfway up the hill we jerked to a halt. It was obvious that the hill was too steep for the donkeys to pull any further.

My father decided to ride Nancy back to Louis Trichardt to ask for help. He returned a few hours later accompanied by an Afrikaans farmer with a driver and a wagon pulled by a span of six oxen. The farmer and my father unhitched the oxen as well as our donkeys, applied the brake and placed boulders behind each wheel to prevent the wagon from rolling back. He then drove the six oxen to the front of our wagon, hitched the ox chain to the donkey chain, shouted, "Hup!" and cracked his long whip. The ox-driver took the lead rope. My father released the brake and at last our wagon jerked free and moved slowly up the hill.

Once at the summit, the farmer and his driver removed the chain from the oxen and hitched up the donkeys once more. My father and farmer, who introduced himself as Mr Bezuidenhout, stood talking for some minutes. My father thanked him and tried to pay him for his help, but he refused to take any payment, saying in broken English, "Mr Mefyous, if I can't help a man and his family in trouble, then I'm no use to mankind. I'm jus virry glet I've been able to help youse. Good luck and totsiens."

My father said later to my mother, "What splendid people these Afrikaans backveld people are. Wherever we've travelled through the bushveld, we've received nothing but kindness, help and guidance from every single one of them. I feel very humbled by their generosity." In the years following the Boer War, the Afrikaners had not been receiving much favourable publicity in England, and since my father had fought against them, he had been used to hearing British army officers condemn the Boers as an evil and treacherous enemy.

We continued trekking westwards for several days. At one point, after a very heavy downpour of rain followed by a thunderstorm, the donkeys were so afraid of the brilliant lightning that they just stopped, huddled together and would not move. We could only sit in the wagon and wait. About half an hour later the storm passed: the menacing, grey clouds rolled away to the east and the sun came out and shone as mercilessly as it had before the storm. The dust road had now been transformed to a muddy riverbed and where the wagon wheels had only recently gripped the rutted surface, they were now stuck fast and the donkeys were standing up to their fetlocks in the mud. We had come to a complete standstill.

Some small herd boys driving their goats down the mountain came to see what was going on. David shouted to them to go to see if they could find some help for us. About an hour later they came back and with them were about six huntsmen, chattering loudly. Each man carried a large panga, a wickedly curved hunting knife shaped something like a sickle. My mother was terrified, sure that we would all be hacked to death, and said urgently, "Stuart, get your gun ready. I don't like the look of these men. Stay with us – don't go to meet them, please." My father said, "No, I don't think they will do us any harm, Mabel. Just keep calm."

The men walked right up to the wagon and greeted my father with, "Shimorena" (greetings). David greeted them and told them of our predicament, whereupon each man went into the veld and cut branches from thorn-bushes. They then tucked the branches firmly round each wheel, while at the same time they scooped as much mud away with their bare hands as they could. David straightened out the ragged line of donkeys. One of the men took the lead rein while others grasped a wheel which they hefted forwards. The combination of the cracking of the whips and the shouting of the men urging the donkeys to pull, made the wagon lurch forwards onto the, by now, submerged branches. It was free at last.

My father thanked everyone very much and gave each man a handful of pipe tobacco. They were so pleased with their reward that they performed an impromptu dance for us, all of them singing in harmony, before they set off for home with their pangas flashing in the brilliant sunlight. Once more in the space of just one day, we had received such spontaneous help and support from men who were not only strangers, but had even been considered to be potential enemies. My mother and father talked about this long into the night, and indeed often in the years that followed.

Several miles further on, we passed a mountain on our right which jutted straight out of the veld, high up into the blue sky. My mother remarked, "What a quiet, lonely and wild-looking mountain. I wonder who on earth lives in such an isolated place."

The next day we drew up outside a small, whitewashed trading store. My father jumped off Nancy and went inside the store to ask if we could outspan under the big thorn trees in front of the shop. He came out again, and said the owner of the store would be quite happy to let us rest, and had even asked us all in for a cup of tea. The donkeys were unhitched and left to graze and David went to join the shop workers in their dinner break.

My father introduced us all to the shopkeeper, then we sat on the verandah and had tea and biscuits. Mr Bell, the owner, was a short, squat, florid man with a very large moustache. He had owned a little shop in Hull before he had emigrated to South Africa several years previously. Mrs Bell was a short, plump Afrikaans tannie with greying hair, which always managed to float in untidy wisps over her forehead and was pulled into a small bun at the back with hairpins sticking out in all directions. Neither of them was well educated but they were very good shopkeepers and had a shrewd business sense.

My father asked Mr Bell what part of England he came from, and he answered in a strong Yorkshire accent, "Hull" and said that he had left England many years ago. Shortly after arriving in Africa, he met his wife, the young daughter of an Afrikaans farmer. They had one son, George, who was a little older than Aubrey. They settled in the Mara area and had been making a good living at their little trading store, since Louis Trichardt was too far away for most people to make the tedious journey by ox or donkey-wagon regularly.

The Bells listened sympathetically to my father then invited us to stay on their farm where we remained for the next few days. They were very kind to us: they gave us goat meat, vegetables, eggs, milk, bread and butter and often invited us to join them in their evening meal. Mr Bell and my father used to sit talking over a glass of beer till the early hours of the morning, discussing among other things, politics and society in England and South Africa.

Mr Bell wasn't able to throw any light on farms for sale in that area. He said it was too wild and parched a district for livestock or crops. No farmer was able to make a good living in the area and in addition, it was in a malaria zone and thousands of people died each year from blackwater fever.

A few days later, Mr Bell introduced my father and mother to Mr and Mrs Chomse who had come to make some purchases from the store. Mr Chomse was a tall, thin man with a very brown, kind face. His wife was in her late thirties, plump, with curly hair and was very pretty and well-dressed. She was Afrikaans and Mr Chomse was of German origin, but both of them spoke English well. They had a baby daughter of about six months old who was sleeping in a blanket tied on to the back of her nanny. Mr Bell told the Chomses that we had been trekking around for six months and had travelled as far as the Blouberg mountain range in search of a farm.

Mrs Chomse said to my father, "That's a long time to be trekking around in the bushveld. You must be very tired. Would you like to come and stay with us till you hear of any farms for sale in the surrounding districts? We have two big, empty rondavels not far from our house and you can come and stay for as long as you like and we'd be very glad to help you in any way we can." Mr Chomse was just as happy to extend the invitation. My parents were only too pleased to accept their hospitality as the strain of six months' trekking through the bushveld was beginning to take its toll on my father who had been an asthmatic for many years.

The next day we packed up the wagon and David inspanned the donkeys again. We all went in to say goodbye to Mr and Mrs Bell and thanked them for their kindness and hospitality during our stay. Aubrey and I were sorry to say goodbye to George because he had given us so many packets of cheap sweets made out of thick mieliemeel porridge and sugar, coloured red, green, yellow and blue.

We arrived at the Chomses' farm about five miles further along the road from Bells' store. The donkeys were led to the front of the rondavels where we unloaded all our bedding, food, goods and chattels. Our stay with Mr and Mrs Chomse was to last for seven months. They were extremely good to us and supplied us with free milk, goat meat, eggs and vegetables and mieliemeel.

David worked as a cook and general servant for Mrs Chomse for three months, then decided that he had been away from home for too long and wanted to go back to see his family at Munnik. My mother and Mrs Chomse packed up a bag containing food and water for his long journey home through the bushveld to Munnik and gave him enough money to buy food along the way. Next morning at dawn, David set off on foot through the veld, a journey home which would last at least three weeks. We all got up early and gave him a good breakfast before he left. He smiled, waved and was soon out of sight in the thick bush. We never heard from him again, and can only hope that he reached his destination safely.

We settled down in the Chomses' rondavels, although my father and mother were still anxious to get their own farm as soon as possible. One day, after a few months had passed, Mr Chomse had driven over to Bells' store for some goods. When he came back, he was excited: he had just heard about a farm for sale about thirteen miles away. My father was very pleased and almost immediately he and Mr Chomse rode over on horseback to view the farm.

When they returned some hours later, they were both in very high spirits and very happy with what they had seen of the farm. When my mother asked whereabouts it was, my father said, "Well, it's about thirteen miles away. It has a mountain and a river flowing through it and some buildings a mile up the mountain. It's recently been occupied by an Afrikaans family."

My mother's response was, "I hope it's not that wild, desolate mountain we passed on our way to Bells' store."

My father replied, "Well, as a matter of fact, my dear, it is." She was quite shocked and said, "Oh, no, Stuart, we can't live up there in that place."

He said reassuringly, "Don't worry – I have great plans for it and I know that we'll be very happy there and soon be very proud of our home. Trust me."

It was a large farm, he said: it was irrigated by the Hout River and it consisted of a mountain and flatland which stretched away to the horizon. A footpath of about a mile connected the buildings to the dirt road that ran along the foothills of the mountain. This was exactly the type of farm we had travelled so far and so long to find.

Next day my father saddled up Nancy and rode to Louis Trichardt, thirty miles away, to negotiate the purchase of the farm with council officials and solicitors and to obtain a bank loan. A few days later, after all the formalities had been completed, he arrived back to tell us that the mountain had been registered as Spitskop in the district of Mara. He was delighted and anxious to get to our new farm as soon as possible.

Soon after this, we began to pack the wagon up again. We assembled the donkeys who, after their six months' holiday, were by now almost too fat to fit into their traces.

All four of us, Aubrey and I in particular, were very excited at the prospect of seeing our own home. In between carrying boxes and provisions onto the wagon in preparation for the last stage of our journey, we scampered around, laughing and playing, and several times my mother called sharply to us to "hurry up with the packing – it will soon be too hot to do any more work."

We left the Chomses one morning, the wagon piled high with our goods and chattels. We were sorry to say goodbye to the Chomses as they had been so kind to us, but we were happy to think we were going to have a home of our own where we could settle after so many months' trekking through the bushveld in search of a farm.

However, in order to manoeuvre the wagon and the donkeys up to the rondavels on the mountainside, my father first had to cut down trees, roll away huge boulders and fill up some of the potholes and ditches in the road. Eventually, bumping and lurching and with the wagon almost overturning at times, we arrived at our new home. It consisted of three thatched mud rondavels and a square hut in the centre. In front of the kitchen there was a small, open verandah. Thick bush grew down the mountain as far as the rondavel walls, which had become a haven for reptiles and snakes. The previous owners, an Afrikaans family, had been unable to make a living; the farm had been repossessed and a few months before we arrived in the area, they had moved on. I can now imagine the surprise of the few black families who had remained on the land at seeing yet another white family determined to tame this inhospitable area.

The donkeys were brought to a halt outside the rondavels. We all climbed down and with the help of some of the men, women and children who lived there, everything was soon off-loaded and put into place. One rondavel became a bedroom, one a dining-room, the third a sitting-room and the square building, my mother decided, was to be our kitchen.

We had brought very little furniture but Mr Bell gave my father boxes and some wood which he used to make cupboards, tables and chairs for our home. Once it had a dab of paint, our furniture soon looked to our inexpert eyes, as good as any in the Chomses' house. We were very proud of it.

Our mountain was unofficially called Spitskop but the farm itself had no name. Since both my parents had lived in Cumberland, they decided that they would like to name this small bit of the African bushveld after their homeland. Consequently, my father wrote to tell Major Hasell who lived in Dalemain, an old manor house near Pooley Bridge in the Lake District, that he would like to call our bushveld farm Dalemain, too. As a boy, my father had spent many happy days with Major Hasell's aunts at Dalemain. Major Hasell wrote back to say he was delighted.

One of my father's first tasks was to appoint a headman, Andries, a very quiet, kind, wrinkled old man who was respected by both my parents as well as by everyone else in the community. Andries lived in one of the huts on the farm with his wife, children and grandchildren, as well as his very old mother, Goba, who was deaf and blind, wrinkled and grey; we thought that she must have been at least ninety years old. She remembered seeing the first white man who ventured into the remote area of the Transvaal where they were living at the time. As nobody in their village had ever seen a white man before, she and her brothers and sisters all ran, screaming and terrified, back to their home to tell their family about the "ghost" they had seen walking about the veld killing animals.

Andries had two wives. His first wife was called Mama Goeba (which meant Mother of her eldest child, Magoeba). She was a small, middle-aged woman, several years younger than Andries. She always appeared to be in a bad temper and we never saw her laugh or smile. She and her daughter-in-law, Makwanna, came to our house every Monday morning to do our weekly washing and ironing. When she was upset, which happened very frequently, she began to talk very loudly and quickly and the rest of the family used to keep well out of her way in order to avoid any confrontation. She ruled her family with a rod of iron. My father said she spoke so quickly that she sounded like a motor-car revving up when she became upset. We nicknamed her "Motorcar" and she answered to the name for many years.

Perhaps to escape from her tyranny, Andries had married a second, younger wife who bore him children of about the same age as Aubrey and I. Their son was called Mankahpa and their daughter, Meofi, and from a very early age, Aubrey and I spent a lot of time playing, hunting, fishing and exploring with them. Meofi was a bright and happy little girl and my best friend on the farm.

We often went down to visit them and to listen to the stories of the adventures that Andries had had in his youth. Meofi and Mankahpa taught us all sorts of useful things: which reptiles were dangerous and poisonous, how to identify the different species of animals and insects, which berries we could eat, and which ones we should avoid. They also taught us how to collect clay from the river banks and mould it into models of animals, carts, people and flowers and how to leave them in the sun to dry out. Meofi and Mankahpa were real artists at this, as these clay models were the only toys they had to play with. Aubrey and I

61

were not as talented, but we were "improving", they used to tell us.

There was a lot of work to be done: first the thick bush had to be cut back. Next my father and some of the locals he employed as farmhands built a four-foot high stone wall with a circumference of about a hundred yards all round the rondavels, to stop the bush from encroaching further. As they worked, they all sang in harmony and Aubrey and I used to stand and listen in admiration to the richness of their voices. After completing the wall, they prepared a large patch of ground for a vegetable garden and built another stone wall round it to keep out wild animals. Soon the seeds that my father planted began to grow into healthy crops – cabbages, cauliflowers, peas, carrots, lettuces and pumpkins. This garden supplied us with all the vegetables we needed throughout the years we lived there.

My mother planted canna lilies against the wall and when they began to bloom they made a brilliant splash of colour: red, yellow pink and white. Fruit trees were planted and gradually the area was transformed from the wilderness it had been when we arrived. There was much to be done: the road had to be rebuilt, and livestock had to be brought back from the market at Louis Trichardt, over roads which were rough, stony, and sandy in the winter, but which swelled to deep mud tracks in the rainy summer months. Kraals were built for the cattle, sties for the pigs, a stable for Nancy, outhouses for the wagon and farm implements, and a granary was erected. We also acquired several kittens from the Chomses.

Every Thursday the rickety mail van that delivered leather mail-bags and supplies from Bells' store to the few isolated inhabitants of the Mara area, drove from Louis Trichardt and along the road leading past our house. My father created a post-box from a sturdy pole nailed to an orange-box. On Tuesdays we left our outward-bound mail in the same orange-box for the postman to collect and take to Louis Trichardt. Every Tuesday and Thursday Aubrey and I ran down to meet the lorry. We filled up the lorry driver's canvas bottle with fresh water, and in return he gave us each sweets or a piece of biltong.

My parents, Aubrey and I drove the donkey cart once a fortnight to Bells' store to buy sugar, tea, rice, flour and mieliemeel. Mr Bell and my parents invariably had long conversations over the counter about England and about the changes that had taken place there since their departure.

The open verandah at the front of our rondavels was surrounded by white stones. Every fortnight some of the women from the kraal collected fresh cow dung which they mixed with water and disinfectant to a soft, sloppy consistency. Crouching down on their hands and knees, they smeared the hard surface of the verandah floor with the green dung mixture and made very attractive swirls and zigzags as they scraped the surplus away with their bare hands. Once the floor was dry, they swept it and it always looked like a pretty green carpet. It never had an unpleasant odour and it kept ants, flies and other insects away.

Aubrey and I used to play very happily with the children of these workers, but we also had another, imaginary playmate. One day Aubrey said, "Let's pretend there's an old man who comes to play with us." I thought this was a really good idea and The Old Man joined in all our games. We held conversations with him and listened to him when he spoke silently back to us. Usually we all played happily together, but sometimes he took Aubrey's side when we had a fight. I would go in crying to my father with my tale of woe, and he would sit me on his knee and say, "Now don't cry; they are very naughty. Just you go out and tell them if they don't let you play I shall come out and send The Old Man away and bring Aubrey inside and won't allow either of them back until they behave themselves." I used to go back to Aubrey, confident and defiant, and gave the message from my father to both him and The Old Man. That always stopped their nonsense and I was then allowed to play again.

Of course, sometimes The Old Man and I would gang up against Aubrey and wouldn't let him play with us. Aubrey would then complain to my mother or father and the same message would be relayed to The Old Man and me. We really enjoyed his company and he remained with us for two years, until he faded away, never to return, when we went to school.

We had lived on the farm for a few months, thinking we were the only English family in that remote backveld area of the Transvaal, when we learned that there were in fact four English families living in more fertile areas within a forty-mile radius of us. These families were the Eastwoods, the Philcoxes, the Archers, and the Rumbles, a family who lived with their two children on the other side of the mountain. Mr and Mrs Eastwood's family had married or were working in Johannesburg, except for their son, Bill, who managed their farm called Buffelspoort. Further along the Soutpansberg were Mr and Mrs Philcox, also farmers. They had two children, Rosemary and Barbara, whom we did not see much as most of the time they were attending Rhoedean, a private school in Johannesburg. Mr and Mrs Archer and their two little girls lived about forty miles from us on the Soutpansberg mountain range on a farm called Kilgobbin. These families had luxurious houses with cream walls, red roofs and had large croquet lawns surrounded by tall blue-gum trees. We used to visit each other occasionally, travelling by donkey cart.

* * * * *

Shortly after my mother and father moved to Dalemain, Herbert and Molly left England for South Africa and both found work in Johannesburg. Norman went to Mozambique to work for a shipping firm. Later on he moved to Kenya. I was not to meet him for nearly forty years.

Robin emigrated to South Africa after Herbert and Molly, once he had completed his schooling. He lived with us on the farm for several months before he went to Johannesburg to work underground in the gold mines. He, Herbert and Molly used to spend their holidays with us and we looked forward to seeing them as we became good friends with Herbert and Robin in particular.

Molly, on the other hand, was very involved with a religious organisation, the Oxford Group, and took it upon herself to try to save me from eternal damnation by walking me down to the river and reading the Bible to me. I found this indescribably boring, but was too afraid of Molly to complain about it. I used to dread having to follow Molly for one of her "quiet times". Apart from this Molly, who had been educated privately at Casterton School in the Lake District, was horrified to hear my strong South African accent. "No, Nancy, it's not thee's a donkey

64

deawn thee, it's 'they-ah's a donkey dahn they-ah'," she would remind me.

As they were so much older than Aubrey and me, Herbert and Robin were very amused by our antics. However, both of them had a Mathews family failing – both of them, like my father, liked to tease us.

Robin used to call me "Flourbags" because I used to run round the farm when I was smaller, wearing knickers made of well-washed calico flourbags, to prevent my good cotton knickers from being torn when I climbed trees or went exploring on Spitskop. I hated being called Flourbags, and I hated Robin even more for doing it, which he persisted in doing, particularly as I reached my teens. Both Herbert and Robin would sometimes come behind us and hold our forearms, then use us as puppets, Herbert making Aubrey box me and Robin making me punch Aubrey in return. This started off as a fun fight, but after a while they started to make us hit each other harder and harder, until when the blows became too much to bear, Herbert and Robin would let go and watch in amusement as a vicious fight developed between Aubrey and me.

Robin, gentle as he was, used to delight in letting me ask politely if anyone else wanted the last biscuit or cake, then saying, "Well, thank you, Nancy, I don't mind if I do," whereupon he would start to eat with exaggerated enjoyment in front of me.

Robin was very handsome and often used to arrive with yet another love of his life on his arm. Girls adored him as he was so kind and handsome. He eventually married the daughter of a Transvaal station master, a redhead with a pronounced South African accent.

My father in some ways was very Victorian: he did not approve because he considered that a station master's daughter was no match for his public-school-educated son, nor did he approve of Robin and his fiancée's snuggling up in front of him, as he considered this to be a very degrading thing to do in public. My father fortunately did not live to witness the sexual freedom of the latter part of the twentieth century.

Herbert was very charming, and also had many girlfriends. He had a much more dynamic personality than Robin and was very meticulous in everything he did, so Aubrey and I had

65

our revenge by tormenting him. We would sometimes deliberately move Herbert's comb or mirror or some small trinket on his dressing-table a fraction out of alignment, just to have the pleasure of seeing him move it back precisely the same fraction into its original place.

CHAPTER 6
DALEMAIN

Dalemain farmhouses and Spitskop Mountain from the south - 1926.

Our farm was the haunt of many species of buck - waterbuck, springbok, kudu, bushbuck and impala; and of bush pigs and leopards, wild cats, baboons, monkeys and snakes. Across the river on the flats roamed porcupines, anteaters, alligators, jackals and hyenas and meerkats.

Hundreds of different species of insects of all shapes, sizes and colours crawled or flew over the veld. We used to squat on the ground and watch the dung beetles as they toiled and pushed their ever-growing dung balls towards their holes in the ground. We were fascinated by a beetle about an inch long with a long, black sting which protruded about a quarter of an inch out of its hard, royal blue back. Aubrey and I used to prod this creature with a stick or a stem of grass, just so that we could hear its high-pitched tee-tee-tee warning us off before it scuttled under a stone or down a hole. We liked to lie on our stomachs on the bare, flat, windswept veld and watch the ant lions, which are soft, brown, hairy creatures the size of a pea. They dug little cone-shaped holes in the ground about two inches deep then they lined the sides of the holes with very fine sand which was intended to trap ants: the powdery dust would give way and the ant would slip to the bottom of the cone, where it was immediately caught by the cunning little ant lion. Almost immediately after digesting its dinner, the ant lion set about digging a trap for its next meal. We used to watch little spurts of dust being flung up all round the sides of the cone before the ant lion paused and waited for another unsuspecting ant to fall into its trap. However we could never actually see the ant lion unless we dug down to the bottom of its hole, and then only when the spurts of dust were coming up. When we uncovered them, the ant lions lay quite still as though dead.

All day long butterflies, brilliant yellow, purple, red, blue and green, fluttered and sparkled amongst the sweet-scented and brilliant flowers, shrubs and trees. Now and again the veld flashed with birds whose plumes were the colour of precious jewels. But for all this brilliance, the cries of these birds were usually harsh and tuneless. The "go-away" bird, or lourie, brownish-grey with a crest on top of its head and a long, black tail feather, had an undulating flight from tree to tree. The local name for them was "Man Thopoldi". Meofi would always wave her hands and arms in imitation of their strange flight and sing a little song:

"Man thopoldi, Geta idi phulu, Vangweh kawena, Va gheta idi phulu, Wavorna." ("Go-away bird, herd your goats, as your families like you herd and look after the goats of their own.") The goats loved going up into the mountain where they climbed up the low acacia trees with their evil thorns, and nibbled at acacia leaves. If the goats strayed too close to the leopard's lair in the krantz, they seldom ignored the go-away bird's warning. People living in the area considered the go-away bird to be a spirit of their forefathers and treated it with a great deal of respect.

The river was full of barbel or catfish, a flat, hard-headed and scaleless fish with long whiskers at the sides of its mouth. Eels writhed and slithered in the river: we did not try to catch them as it was hard to distinguish between them and the black, poisonous water-snakes.

No-one hunted in that area as it was so remote that very few people knew about the abundance of game. Eventually, though, word spread and hunters began to come to ask permission to shoot on the farm. All of them were met with a very polite but definite, "No hunting or game shooting on my farm," from my father.

Sometimes tired, footsore men would come to our house to beg for food, water and shelter for the night. My parents never refused them hospitality: these travellers ate with the farmhands and were provided with blankets and bedding in an outhouse. As soon as they felt fit, they continued their journey. Some of them were looking for long-lost relations or seeking work, and some were escaping from disease or hardship.

One blistering summer's day a man dressed in badly torn trousers several sizes too big and wearing sandals made of car tyres tied up with thongs, hobbled up, footsore, hungry and weary. Aubrey and I ran in to call my father, who came out and spoke to the stranger, who was so exhausted that he could hardly speak and fell asleep on the ground in the shade of the rondavel. When he awoke he was given food and water and he asked if my father had any work for him on the farm. We had so many people already working there that my father had to say that there was no work. My mother asked him then if he could cook. "Yes, missi, I cook," he replied, and with that he was hired as our cook/houseboy, as black domestic male workers were then called in South Africa. He said his name was John and he had come from Blantyre in Nyasaland, thousands of miles away, to look for a good home. He worked happily for us for twelve years. Seventy years later, Aubrey and I still spoke affectionately about "Old John" as he appeared to us. He had a face of the darkest ebony which was pitted and scarred very badly from smallpox which must have made him very ill in his youth. He was one of the finest, most honest, kindest and gentlest men I have ever known, and because of this, nobody noticed his scarring.

One morning Old John knocked at the door and said, "Preez, Baas and Missi, you come rook my Bludder." He habitually turned all "L"s into "R"s and all "R"s into "L"s. We went outside to see, sitting beside the water trough under a tall thorn tree, a man who was obviously very exhausted. He looked like Old John though he was younger and much more handsome. He stood up, smiled at us and said, "Good morning, Missi and Baas." My parents replied, "Good morning," then my father asked John what he wanted and John said, "He want work for you, preez, he velly good man." My father said, "You know, John, I have no work for anybody at present." He then put his hand to his chin and, after a moment's reflection he added, "Well, look, John, take him to your room and let him rest for a couple of days and I'll talk it over with the Missis and see what we can do for him."

When John came back to us he thanked my father very much and told us how his brother, Dado, had walked all the way from Nyasaland to join him. My father wondered how he could have traced John from so many hundreds of miles away.

My father went inside to ask my mother's opinion. They eventually agreed that since Dado seemed to be like his brother, a good and kind man, they would find some work for him. Besides, as all the other farmhands had been born in the area, Dado would be company for John.

John was called and asked to bring his brother to the house. They both stood anxiously waiting for the decision, and eventually my father said, "Right then, Dado. Well, the Missis and I have decided you can stay. Your job will be to look after the vegetable garden and the flowers and sweep up round the house every day, but above all, keep the garden full of vegetables and well cared for and well watered." John and Dado both smiled broadly, put their hands together on their foreheads and bowed several times. Dado remained with us for many years. He was a diligent and quiet worker and like John, he became one of our best friends.

Aubrey and I often used to join John and Dado as they sat round their fire outside their hut while they were cooking their mieliemeel, meat and vegetables for their evening meal. They told us wonderful stories about their dangerous journey on foot from Nyasaland, over high mountains and hot, arid, flatland where every step had to be trodden with care in order to avoid snakes.

They spun such vivid tales of their mammoth walk and the adventures they had had that Aubrey and I were spellbound and spent many evenings listening, enthralled. Dado in particular was an excellent story-teller and painted vivid pictures of all his encounters. They had washed their clothes in rivers and then sat on the bank while their clothes dried out. They had swum such broad, swift-running rivers that on occasion, they had both nearly drowned.

Often they had made ten-mile detours; they had slept in trees at night, carrying a panga and a strong forked stick to protect themselves from the lions, leopards and cheetahs that roamed about the vast veld. Sometimes, they told us, lions or hyenas used to smell them as they sat in the branches of the tree and sit waiting all night underneath for John and Dado to either fall out or climb down.

Once, when John was resting in a tree, a leopard started to climb the tree trunk. It got so close that the only thing John could do was to lash out with his panga and split its head open. The smell of fresh blood attracted hordes of hyenas and jackals and while the leopard was barely alive but defenceless, they tore it to pieces. By daylight no trace of it was left and the scavengers, now with bulging bellies, had gone, too, so John was able to climb down and run away.

Danger came, too, in the form of local villagers. Some regarded John and Dado as intruders and were so hostile to them that the brothers often had to hide all day to avoid being hacked to death.

The rivers presented danger of a different kind: the ever-present menace of crocodiles. At one point a large crocodile crawled very close to Dado and opened its jaws wide: Dado thrust his forked stick straight into its eyes. The pain caused it to turn; it thrashed around and churned up the water, and this gave Dado a chance to reach the riverbank and climb out of the river, exhausted.

John and Dado had to forage for wild fruit and dig up the roots of trees and plants. They used knobkerries to kill rabbits which they skinned and cut up. They then hung the skins out to dry on the white needle-shaped thorns high up in the trees.

* * * * *

The years passed. One very bright, hot moonlit night, Aubrey and I were sitting round the fire, listening to John and Dado's tales. Aubrey had a .22 rifle on his knee, which he had used earlier that evening to shoot a rabbit for John and Dado. Dado was sitting on a big boulder beside the fire, occasionally stirring their stew and the mieliemeel in the pot over the big, black tripod on the fire.

He was talking to us about guns and wanted to know which "thing" we pulled to shoot. Aubrey emptied the magazine first, and said, "Oh, you just aim at the thing you want to shoot and then pull the trigger back like this, look – it's easy." To demonstrate this, Aubrey put his finger on the trigger and pulled it back. Just as he did this, Dado leaned forward to see what Aubrey

71

was doing. There was a loud crack then a thud as Dado fell with a groan off the boulder he was sitting on, onto the ground. Fine red dust powdered the air, then settled on the earth and on the trickle of blood, leaving everything very still in its wake. Dado had been shot dead through the temple.

Old John was devastated. Aubrey and I were stunned. My father ran over immediately to find out where the gunshot had come from. He stood transfixed when he saw Dado on the ground, then he said quietly, "What happened?" and almost hysterical, we told him. He said, "I'll have to ride over to Bells' store to telephone for the police." He set off immediately down the road on horseback with a storm lamp in front of the saddle, picking his way along the dark, stony road. He returned a few hours later and said that the police were on their way to the farm to interview John, Aubrey and me, but wouldn't be able to reach our farm till late morning as they had to ride several miles from the police station at Mara Sending.

Next day the police arrived, questioned all of us and Aubrey in particular for a long time, then spoke to Old John who assured the detective that the whole incident had been an accident and he felt no anger towards Aubrey at all. A few days later we travelled to Mara Sending police station where Old John solidly testified to the magistrate that Aubrey had no intention of shooting Dado. The next day, Dado's funeral took place: a ceremony attended by Old John, Andries, my father and two other farmhands. John spoke a few words, and my father said, "Goodbye, Dado, may you rest in peace. God be with you." John wrapped Dado in his blankets with all his clothes. Dado was buried at the foot of the mountain, with a large stone to mark his grave. Dado's death left a very big gap in all our lives – and especially in Old John's.

* * * * *

Old John missed Dado very much. Local villagers in the Mara district spoke dialects of Sepedi or Venda, neither of which John could speak. He was, however, able to speak a little of what is known as Fanagolo. We all felt very sorry for Old John who sat alone in his room or outside beside his fire. We hoped that someone else from his part of the world would come along one day to keep him company.

About three months after Dado's tragic death, Old John came to my parents on Saturday morning and said, "Preez, Missi and Baas, me want go fetchum wife this afternoon." Both my father and mother were very pleased for him and Old John was smiling broadly. My father asked where the bride-to-be lived, how old she was and how long he had known her.

Still smiling broadly, Old John said, "Oh, she young wife, I find her this morning sitting on Berrs' shop stoep, she arone and I ask her to be my wife and she say yes stlaight away. So me go fetchum this afternoon, she got em one boy; he thlee years old. She Venda gir'." My father asked John where he was going to collect her. John said, "Oh, she waiting for me on Berrs' stoep."

My father said, "We're really pleased for you, John. Take the donkey cart to bring them back. Look, here's some money to buy them some blankets." He handed John a few coins, a pair of his own trousers, a shirt, a jacket and a tie to celebrate the occasion. The shirt, trousers, jacket and a blue straw hat that had belonged to my mother were too big for him, but Old John did not seem to mind. The donkeys were quickly caught and inspanned in the cart and he drove off proud, happy and resplendent in his new clothes.

When he returned a few hours later, his new wife, Maria, and her little son, Malivadja, were at his side. John proudly introduced them to us. "Baas, Missi, here Malia, my wife." Maria was obviously much younger than Old John, and very shy; she smiled broadly and held her left hand in front of her eyes as we greeted her. Malivadja, dressed in the same way as all the local children, wore only a little piece of rabbit skin. My mother had hunted out some old clothes for both Maria and Malivadja. She gave these to John, who led his new bride away to his room. He beamed with pleasure and pride at his new family and his enhanced status as a breadwinner.

Aubrey and I were sent over with some provisions, vegetables and meat for their meal, and told to come straight back again after we had delivered the goods.

Maria had never worked as a domestic servant and could not speak a word of English; nor was my mother able to speak any Venda. Nevertheless, she arranged with John for Maria to help with the washing up and with any of John's other domestic duties. This arrangement worked very well for several months. Meofi and Mankahpa often came round to play with Malivadja and sometimes took him down to their hut for the day.

A few months after Maria's arrival at the farm, John announced to my mother that Maria was pregnant. My mother lightened Maria's workload. During the next few months, my mother was kept busy making baby clothes and maternity dresses. Eight months later early one morning when John brought our tea, he proudly announced that Maria had given birth to a daughter during the night.

The following afternoon we went down to visit Maria and her daughter, who seemed so small and so well wrapped up in blankets, that we could barely see her in the darkened hut. My mother found her tiny hand and placed half a crown into it. The little hand immediately clutched the coin tight – much to Maria's joy, as that was a sign of luck, she said.

John and his family were very happy. Each morning Maria, with the little baby firmly tied onto her back, helped him with the housework. However, one Sunday morning, when the baby was eight weeks old, Old John came to the house. He was very upset and near to tears. He asked my mother to "Come quick preez – the baby is velly sick." My mother hurried out to the hut and was horrified at the sight she saw.

Winter nights in the Northern Transvaal are very cold, so there was always a hollow in the centre of all the huts where the family kept a fire burning twenty-four hours a day, to heat their home and for cooking. The whole family slept under blankets arranged on mats round the fire. In the evening, the men would often sit round the fire drinking their beer, a thick brown liquid made of ground corn mixed with water and left in the sun to ferment for a few days. The beer was stirred daily and when it was fully brewed, it was strained through wire mesh and taken into the huts where it was poured into big, round earthenware pots. Dried reeds cut into six inch lengths were strewn over the beer, to cover it until it was fully fermented and ready for drinking. This beer was very potent and was enjoyed by both men and women.

That night Maria had been drinking so heavily that she had not noticed that her baby had rolled off the mat and right onto the smouldering embers. Maria had been oblivious to her baby's screams. The baby had been burnt so severely down her left side that some of her fingers and toes had been lost.

My mother, shocked and angry with Maria who was still very drunk, ran back to the house. She took wads of cotton wool, bandages and lotions for the baby's extensive burns and twice a day for the next three weeks she continued to dress them. Eventually the raw flesh began to heal.

Unfortunately just at this time my mother, father, Aubrey and I had to leave for Pietersburg hundreds of miles away to attend my father's regular examination by the British army doctors for his military pension. Before we left, my mother gave Maria enough cotton wool, bandages, lotions and ointment to enable her to continue dressing the wounds twice daily until we returned a week later. Maria promised to follow her instructions exactly.

When we arrived home, Old John was there at the gate to meet us. His eyes were heavy-lidded and red as he told us that the baby had died that morning. Maria had failed to follow my mother's instructions, the bandages had become wet and dirty and the burns had all turned septic. My mother felt sorry for Maria, but she was also very angry with her for being so careless and told her so. Maria was inconsolable.

A few months later Old John brought the news that Maria was pregnant again. Both he and Maria seemed very happy, and we were all pleased for them. It had been a very cruel way for Maria to realise the folly of heavy drinking, but she drank no beer from then on, and their second little girl, Majee, was strong and healthy. This time the baby was well cared for and Majee grew into a happy, active little girl.

Several babies were born on the farm while we lived there. They were all breast-fed and generally grew into strong, sturdy children. When the babies were about ten days old, their mothers would sit down on the ground just outside their huts. They placed some specially prepared, very finely ground sorghum

75

porridge in a calabash then mixed it with soured milk to a very sloppy consistency. They wedged the tiny baby firmly between their thighs with his head between their breasts, cupped their left hand just below the baby's chin and with their right hand full of the diluted mixture, poured some porridge into the baby's mouth. If the baby did not open his mouth, his mother would pinch his little nose, which meant he had to open his mouth to breathe. Each time he did that, a large mouthful of porridge was gulped down, very often the wrong way, which made him splutter and become very anxious. It always frightened me to see them fling their arms rigidly out in a terrible effort to breathe, while their mothers just sat quite calmly pouring porridge down their throats and singing a lullaby.

When the bowl of porridge had been swallowed, spluttered and coughed down, the infant's mother wiped his face and bulging little stomach, held him under his arms facing her and jumped him up and down vigorously a few times to shake the porridge down. She then put him to her breast and tied him securely in a goatskin or blanket round her back where he usually slept soundly for several hours. This ritual was repeated every morning for a few months.

The women local to our area were known elsewhere as "lazy women" – there was some irony in this since they bore the brunt of the work in the village, while their menfolk, when not working on the farm, often sat in the shade, drank beer and then slept for the rest of the day. Women began their day by making porridge for breakfast, feeding and washing the small children and babies, cleaning the huts and grinding the corn, which was a communal task. They rubbed the grains of corn between a large, flat stone which had been made hollow by the constant grinding of smaller, round stones, knelt down and placed the corn on a flat part of the stone then moved the grinding stone forwards and backwards. Each forward movement caught several grains of corn which were ground ever finer, then pushed into a calabash at the opposite end of the grinding stone. The women always worked to the rhythm of a lusty song.

Since mielie pips were much larger, they were put into a hollowed-out tree trunk and ground by two women who thumped round-ended poles about six feet long onto the mielies in the hollow of the stump. As they worked, both women sang loudly and harmoniously. Tied to their backs with a goatskin, their babies slept soundly, their heads rocking from side to side in time with the stamping.

When the corn had been ground, the women went to fetch water from the river a mile or more away. For this they used very large clay pots which they balanced on their heads. At the riverside, the women bathed their babies, fed them and laid them down under a shady bush while they washed themselves and the other small children who were splashing happily in the river. The women then washed their clothes, laid them out on the riverbank to dry, folded them, tied them into a bundle, and then tied both the bundle and their baby onto their backs. They lifted the pots of water onto their heads and made their way home. Short pieces of reed growing on the riverbanks were placed on top of the pots to prevent the water from spilling out. Their washing was hung over thorn-bushes near their huts, where it quickly dried out in the sun.

Once a week, when they had finished their morning chores, they walked to their local store to buy soap, salt, blankets, matches and any other provisions they needed. Their babies slept peacefully on their backs for most of the journey. If one awoke and became fretful, his mother would loosen the goatskin or blanket that held him, shift his head round under her armpit and swing her breast round to meet his mouth as she continued to trudge along the road. Once the baby was satisfied, he was pushed back to his original position in the goatskin or blanket. His mother would continue trudging home with a ten-pound sack of mielies on her head, her baby on her back, and carrying the week's shopping in her hands. Her husband, who would often have been socialising or sleeping for a good part of the day, woke in time to enjoy a hearty meal.

Young girls, too, played their part in caring for both the very old and the very young. Meofi's grandmother, Goba, suffered from what was probably osteoporosis and was bent almost double. We often saw Meofi walking backwards and pulling Goba along, both of them holding onto a short, stout stick. This was particularly useful as Goba needed to take frequent trips to the veld to empty her bowels and bladder.

Early on summer mornings we used to wake at dawn and sit drinking coffee out on the open stoep. We loved to listen to the wakening calls of the animals, birds and frogs as they greeted the new day.

We heard the birds' cries: the guinea-fowl down by the river and the fish eagles, who challenged each other with their distinctive cry, a warning that they had staked their claim to fishing rights on a particular stretch of river.

We watched the sun rise over the eastern horizon beside Bristows Koppies. It cast shades of vivid orange, red, yellow, mauve, pink and blue in an arc across the sky, and as it shone over the wispy, early morning mists that were slowly climbing up over bush and rock, it tinted the mountain green, brown and pink.

On the southern horizon in front of us we watched fascinating mirages appear: long, blue mountain ranges with high peaks which pierced the pale blue early morning sky, with large, shimmering blue lakes appearing at their foothills. My father told us they looked just like the beautiful mountains and lakes of Switzerland.

Eventually, our Swiss mountains became distorted and disappeared altogether, while the lakes also began to dry up and fade away, leaving only the flat, orange-shimmering horizon. Our magical glimpse into Switzerland had disappeared with the mirages. Fifteen years later, Aubrey viewed the mountains of Switzerland from afar when he flew near the Swiss border as a rear gunner on bombing raids in the Second World War, and I admired them from the air as I travelled from England to visit Aubrey in South Africa sixty years later.

Once the magic of daybreak had passed, it was time for us to begin our daily activities. We raced down to the hen run, climbed up the tall thorn tree where the hens were all roosting and shook the branches vigorously till the last loudly-protesting hen and rooster flapped awkwardly and noisily onto the ground. We then quietly shinned down the tree before my father came to investigate the cause of all the noise.

After making early morning coffee, my father would then go into the kitchen and cook temptingly sizzling breakfasts for us all: ham and eggs, tomato, sausage, brinjals and fried bread. After breakfast the farm work began. First the cows were brought into the kraal to be milked. Their horns were tied to posts and their back legs were tied together to stop them from kicking while they were milked by our farmhands who squatted on the ground with buckets held between their knees.

The rich, creamy milk was carried in cans up to the house where my mother was waiting to supervise the separating. Some milk was set aside for us and for the farmhands. As the rest of the milk was separated, cream poured out of the top spout and skimmed milk out of the lower spout. The cream was collected in five-gallon cans on Tuesdays and taken down to the post box where it was picked up by a lorry and transported to the dairy in Louis Trichardt. The skimmed milk was taken to the pigsties and poured into the pig troughs. On Wednesdays my mother made the cream into butter. She used a metal churn with a handle which twisted the churn round and round till the thick cream coagulated into butter. The churn was then opened up and the rich butter removed with two wooden oblong butter pats and moulded into one-pound squares. She then placed these squares safely under mosquito netting on a slab of cement in the larder near a south-facing window where the butter kept well for days.

We kept several dozen pigs, mostly large blacks or large whites. After being fed with meal and milk each morning, the pigs were let out of the sties and went to root about on the veld nearby. They were brought back again before sunset. Aubrey and I waited at the gate of the pigsty every morning. As the pigs ran out grunting and squealing, we would each grab the biggest one we could see and jump onto its back, then race down the long, steep road to the bottom of the hill. Staying on the back of a pig was not easy. It would lurch forward onto its front feet, then bump back onto its hind legs, so that we were continually thrown backwards and forwards between tail and shoulder. There was little to hold on to so we tucked our bare feet tightly behind its ears; we laid one hand flat on its back, while the other hand held on grimly to its tail. Pig riding was such fun and we were laughing so much that as often as not we were catapulted off its back long before we reached the bottom of the hill. Whenever my mother discovered that we had been riding pigs, she would not allow us into any part of the rondavels until we had been thoroughly bathed in disinfectant and changed our clothes.

Like some farms in the Transvaal of the nineteen-twenties, we provided the community of farmhands who lived on the farm with free meat and milk, as well as mielies and sorghum seeds for cultivation; my father also loaned them our plough and oxen to enable them to till their own land.

Meofi, Mankahpa, Aubrey and I often walked to the lower slopes of Spitskop to pick morogo, a leafy plant that grew quite profusely close to the ground. The leaves were quite small, green on the upper side and purple underneath, but when boiled with a little water and salt, and with a knob of butter added to the cooked leaves, this became a very tasty dish. Like spinach, it boiled down very quickly, so we had to pick from early in the morning until lunch time in order to have enough for a bucket for Aubrey and me and calabashes full for Meofi and Mankahpa.

My parents were both very fond of listening to music, so on one of our journeys by donkey cart to Louis Trichardt, my mother and father purchased among other items, a gramophone and some ten-inch, black, shiny records. These included Humoresque, Jerusalem, The Lost Chord, I'll Take You Home Again Kathleen, My Little Grey Home In The West, Nellie Melba singing By The Waters of Minnetonka, Yeomen of England, The Lord's Prayer, God Save The King and songs my father had sung in the Great War such as It's a Long Way to Tipperary and Keep the Home Fires Burning. They had also bought a few children's records which included The Laughing Policeman. We loved that and played it over and over again.

Just after we had bought the gramophone and records, we raced down to Andries's hut to bring Meofi and Mankahpa so that they could hear The Laughing Policeman. Aubrey wound up the gramophone, put the record on the turn-table, positioned the needle and shut the lid. When Meofi and Mankahpa came into the room they were met by the loud laughter from the record. They looked round and saw that the noise was coming from the closed box. They were terrified and ran away down the road, screaming at the top of their voices, "A spook in a box is laughing at us!" A very worried Andries then came to the house to investigate. We showed him into the room where the box was still laughing loudly. He was nervous and walked round and round the box to try to find the "man" while repeatedly uttering, "Tso!" and "Iphi?" (Goodness, where is he?)

We opened up the lid and explained it was the needle going round and round on the record that was causing all the noise. This explanation satisfied Andries. He went outside and spoke to his children for a while. Eventually Meofi and Mankahpa came back very gingerly into the room. After they had overcome their initial fear, they really enjoyed coming up to listen to the "singing box" – especially the "laughing spook", which caused such amusement that they both completely drowned out the song with their loud guffaws. No matter how many times we played the record to them, their reaction was the same: they clasped their heads with their hands and screamed with laughter as they rolled over and over on the floor.

* * * * *

Mr and Mrs Behrens were a friendly old Afrikaans couple who lived with their grandchildren, Nora and Lionel, on the mountain next to ours. The Behrens's teenage daughter, Isa, had brought terrible disgrace on the family by becoming pregnant while she was still a young girl. To avoid any further embarrassment to either herself or her parents, she left home and went to live in Johannesburg where she was safely delivered of twins, Nora and Lionel. Nora was a very pretty girl about the same age as me and we became very good friends. Mrs Behrens occasionally visited our farm and taught my mother useful skills such as how to make soap and sausages. Once she had mastered soap-making, my mother and Motorcar regularly made soap from rendered-down pig fat. I often watched them standing outside and stirring the soap in a pan balanced on a large tripod over an open fire. The mixture was left to cool, then was cut into slabs, put onto the kitchen shelves and left to dry out for a few weeks. Motorcar and her family used this soap liberally as she said it was far better than any soap bought from the shop.

81

In return for teaching her these skills, my mother would not let Mrs Behrens go away empty-handed, and sent her back home with home-baked cakes, bottled fruit, or whatever happened to be in the larder at the time.

Occasionally, when Mr Behrens shot a waterbuck on his farm, he brought us some biltong which he made by washing strips of raw meat, rubbing them well with salt and herbs then hanging them up in a hot and preferably windy place to dry for about two weeks. We loved biltong, which is now much more widely available in other countries.

My mother and father used to hang out the biltong to dry in the big thorn tree behind the rondavels. Old John and a young boy would climb up the tree and suspend the strips of meat protected by fly-proof netting on the highest branches so that the dogs could not reach it. On one occasion, three days after the meat had been hung outside, my mother came inside and said that all the biltong had vanished. Old John called my father and said, "Rook, baas, you reopard you came stear birtong (biltong) rast night." John showed him the unmistakable footprints of a leopard and the claw marks on the tree trunk. The leopard had come so stealthily in the night that not even the dogs had heard him.

* * * * *

One sultry morning when I was about seven years old, we were sitting on the verandah having our morning coffee when my father remarked how still and quiet it was. He looked westwards and suddenly said, "What's that?" We turned our heads towards the direction of his gaze and saw a long, low, dark cloud that was stretching across the south western horizon and slowly growing bigger as it rose high in the sky. At first we thought it was a large thundercloud, but as it grew, it looked more like a locust swarm, although my father said it had risen much higher than locusts were able to fly. We watched the cloud roll across the veld for about an hour. Suddenly my father said, "Good Lord, it's a dust storm! Go inside the rondavels, close all the doors and shut the windows." We put the cats and dogs into an empty hut, covered the beds and all our food and kitchen cupboards with sheets, then we went into the bedroom to sit out the storm.

The birds had stopped chirping. It grew darker and darker as the dust storm approached, blotting out the sun completely. The atmosphere grew more oppressive and ominous. We tied wet handkerchiefs over our noses and mouths. We had no idea how long the dust storm was going to last as everything outside was just a blur of ochre dust which covered trees, flowers and rocks – we could not even see the road or the mountain just behind us.

I remember thinking how quiet and eerie it was. There was not even a breath of wind as the thick blanket of red and yellow dust fell silently on everything.

After a couple of hours, it began to get lighter and we could once more see the mountain. My father opened the bedroom door and looked out at this strange sight. Everything had been painted a reddy-ochre: trees, garden, roads, thatched roofs, as well as the dust sheets we had put down inside.

We let out the animals. The dogs sniffed and sneezed as they ran round the farmyard. My father said there must have been a violent sand storm in either the Namib or the Kalahari Desert, and that a wind had whipped up the dust and carried it high into the sky for hundreds of miles.

My mother and Old John were kept busy for days after this, washing and cleaning everything.

Aubrey with Donkeys & water cart 1929

CHAPTER 7
RECREATION

Initially, our only source of water at Dalemain was Hout River, though in the rain-free winter months even that dried up into pools which became brown and muddy, so we all had to use water very sparingly. We dammed up one of the larger pools in order to provide ourselves with water for cooking, drinking and cleaning. From here each day, the donkey cart transported it in ten-gallon cans, to the house. In order for it to be drinkable, water had to stand before being strained and boiled to let the sediment sink. This was time-consuming, inconvenient and unsatisfactory so eventually my father hired a water diviner to see if he could find water near to the rondavels.

The diviner, a sun-tanned Englishman who had lived in South Africa for many years, arrived one morning, dressed in a khaki safari suit and a battered trilby hat. He held a forked metal instrument parallel to the earth while he walked round the area near the house for several hours. For a while this did not seem to produce any result. He was almost ready to abandon his search when suddenly the metal rod swung right down and pointed just in front of him.

84

He told my father he was sure that if we sunk a borehole on that spot we would find a good supply of water. Soon afterwards, engineers arrived in ox wagons laden with drills, pipes, rods and engines. The diviner showed the engineer the location of the water and left the following day, just as the excavation began. Soil, rocks, boulders and shale were brought up and piled in a heap alongside the hole. The noise was deafening and continued for over a week as the metal ground deeper into the rock.

The drill eventually reached a depth of one hundred and fifty feet but still only dry rock and shale were being brought to the surface. The engineer began to despair and told my father, "It's no good, Mr Mathews, there is no water down there, not even a sign of it. All I'm finding are layers of solid rock." After a discussion with the engineer and the drillers, it was decided to ask the diviner to return, which he did a few days later. He held his divining rod directly above the shaft and again the rod pointed straight down the shaft, just as it had previously.

The diviner then said, "There is water, and it's a very strong stream. It's not very much further down – I suggest you drill for about another twenty feet." He fanned his face with his trilby hat and sat down to watch the drilling.

Work started again; the pistons and the plunger hammered down through the rock layers and brought up fragments of dry rock. At a depth of about a hundred and seventy feet, the plunger came up once again but this time the earth it brought up was slightly damp. Each time the plunger surfaced, the soil it brought up appeared to be a little wetter, until amidst shouting and clapping, the plunger appeared full of muddy water. The drill had struck an underground river at last. Everybody was delighted: the engineers clapped and shouted, my mother and father hugged and kissed each other, my father shook hands with the engineers and the diviner, the diviner raised his hat in salute, and Old John, Andries, Meofi, Mankahpa, Aubrey and I danced and sang round the borehole. Pipes were immediately connected and put down the shaft, the windmill was hoisted into place just above the borehole, and the base of the windmill was cemented firmly in place.

85

We all watched and waited with bated breath as the engines released the chain that allowed the windmill blades to turn round and pump up the water, but they did not move, as there was no wind to turn them.

The windmill

For several days we prayed that the wind would get up soon. Patiently we waited but the air was still, and nothing stirred. Then late one morning, Old John knocked at the sitting-room door and said to my mother and father, "Preez, Baas and Missi, you come see quick." He ran round the corner of the rondavel and pointed to the windmill. Sure enough the blades were turning slowly in the light breeze. The breeze strengthened into a wind and the blades started to turn faster and faster till the plunger was pumping up and down frenziedly. At first it brought up muddy water, then the water began to lighten in colour and eventually, clear water was gushing out of the pipe into a three-thousand-gallon tank which had been erected at the outflow. Soon water overflowed from the tank and was filling the trough alongside. This trough was to supply the animals with drinking water in the hot, dry months. There was to be no more filling up cans from the muddy river, and no more boiling the water.

The village women came every morning to fill up their clay pots, calabashes and empty five-gallon paraffin tins. The windmill, manufactured by Samsons in England, was the biggest mechanical giant that we had seen. A tall metal ladder supported the huge blades and the platform which stood many feet above the ground. One of the blades extended into a slightly longer tail, which swung round in the wind, rather like a weathercock. The whole construction was supported on a huge concrete block.

The windmill was turned off before we went to bed, as very strong winds at night sometimes made the blades spin round so fast that the tank overflowed and hundreds of gallons of water were wasted. At night when the machine was left on, the tail and blades revolved in the wind and made an eerie noise that echoed and re-echoed up the mountain in the darkness. It always sounded to me like a lost soul calling. Often it would wake me during the night and frighten me; I used to creep into my mother's bed for comfort.

The windmill became Aubrey's and my favourite toy. We used to climb up the ladder till we got to the platform at the top, when we would wait for the breeze to blow the blades round until the tail was positioned just over the platform. We would then stretch up, hold on to the top of the tail and swing wildly as we were blown round and round a hundred feet above the ground. We held on till we were over the platform again, then we released our grip and dropped down on to the platform. We took it in turns to play this exciting game, which we kept secret from my parents. One day, however, my mother happened to see me flying round high above the ground. She instantly called us both inside and found out just how regularly we had been doing this. Unfortunately for us, this death-defying activity was instantly curtailed and we were not allowed to climb the windmill blades again.

* * * * *

On Tuesdays, my parents, Aubrey, three farmhands and I would often set off in the donkey wagon for Louis Trichardt where we stayed overnight in Hotel Louis. The next morning we rose very early and went to the livestock market where my father bought and sold pigs, cattle and goats. After some haggling, he would strike a deal and we would eventually be ready for the journey back home. Pigs were loaded, squealing and struggling, up onto the wagon while two of the men drove the cattle back. My father took the reins of the donkey wagon and the third man sat in the wagon and looked after the pigs. After a long, slow, bumpy, and noisy drive home we were relieved to be able to jump off the wagon and watch the pigs being unloaded and driven into their sties. The cattle meanwhile were driven down to the river to drink and graze after their long and exhausting walk.

My father also sometimes travelled to Louis Trichardt to buy farm implements – such things as a wood planer, nails and hammers, saddles and bridles. This always entailed a three-day round trip by donkey cart and also included an overnight stop in the hotel.

One morning very early he left with Andries. My father had an air of mystery about him, and no matter how much we pestered him, he would not say where he was going or why. My mother, too, was just as annoyingly reticent. On the third day when my father arrived back at the farm, Aubrey and I ran down to the gate to meet him and Andries. Tied with a long rope to the back of the donkey were three horses and two Basutoland ponies. My father had chosen Dandy, one of the horses, for himself. Dandy was a really handsome retired racehorse and his chestnut coat shone like burnished gold in the sun. He had suffered a swollen hock in a racing accident and could consequently race no longer.

My father unhitched the two ponies and called us over. He handed me a rope for the mare, Nellie, and he handed Charley's rope to Aubrey. We were really excited, and wanted to ride straight away, but my father insisted that we should learn properly. He was an excellent horseman and he set a very strict test for us to pass before he would allow us to take charge of our own ponies. He built a course for us and made us practise various manoeuvres until we could achieve them within specified time limits. In addition to this, he made sure we were proficient in walking, tripling, trotting and cantering, both bareback and in the saddle, and he made us prove we were able to handle a horse that was bucking or shying. Before long we were cantering and galloping all over the farm and were perfectly at home in the saddle. We used to groom Charley and Nellie every day and after a while they were so used to us that they trotted across when they saw us.

My father was very proud of Dandy and kept his saddle and bridle soft and well oiled. The only time I heard raised voices between my parents was one day just before they set off on a visit to one of the neighbours. My mother called out, "Stuart, have you seen my primrose blouse? I can't find it anywhere and I've looked all over."

My father appeared, looking very sheepish and guilty. "I didn't think you'd wear it again," he said, by way of explanation. He had used my mother's best silk blouse which had been sent over from England, to polish his beloved cowboy saddle. Nothing but the best would do!

One afternoon, a few weeks later, my father set out once again for Louis Trichardt. As usual after a couple of days he arrived back and called Aubrey and me over to see what he had brought for us. We opened the bag and out wriggled a soft white head, two small ears and a small, snuffly nose. It was the dearest little puppy we'd ever seen, white all over excepting for a black patch over one eye, another patch on his ear and a third at the base of his tail. My father said his name was Crusoe. Crusoe was a cross between a bull terrier and a bulldog and in the years that followed he became our playmate, our constant companion, our protector and our friend.

* * * * *

On balmy summer nights when the moon was bright and when my father and mother were sitting outside on the verandah, watching the stars and chatting, we used to go down to collect Meofi and Mankahpa and play hide-and-seek and tiggy-you're-it. Crusoe always joined in the fun and was able to hide and seek much better than we did. He barked and jumped about excitedly, and altogether we all made such a noise that the combination of our shouting and Crusoe's yapping disturbed the sleeping baboons up in the mountain and made them bark even more loudly in protest about being wakened so rudely in the night.

There is little twilight in South Africa as darkness quickly follows the setting sun, when the daytime creatures have all found shelter for the night, and when the nocturnal creatures of the veld begin to stir.

This was the time when we often sat out on our verandah to enjoy the balmy evening air. The searing heat of the day had gone and we watched the glittering stars appear across the skies. My father taught us where to look for the Plough, the Bear,

Orion's Belt, the Southern Cross and the Seven Sisters. It was so interesting that I decided I was going to be an astronomer when I grew up. The huge, golden moon rose over the horizon and climbed slowly into the heavens. We loved this time of day. Our paraffin lamps were lit and placed all around the verandah floor. They helped to keep the frogs, crickets, lizards and small animals away, as well as the snakes that liked to slither out in order to warm themselves on the hot ground after hiding from the sun's intense rays under stones and bushes.

My father was a gifted story-teller and could hold a room full of people enthralled with stories of his many exploits in the war and his travels in Canada and Europe. I liked to listen to the tales of his boyhood and his adventures in the Boer and First World wars, and about the time he spent working as a cowboy in Canada. When his sister, Kate, visited us in Wigton many years later, she told us how Stuart, surrounded by a mesmerized audience, would invariably be found in the centre of every party. He had the gift of drawing people to him. This was, after all, the man who had charmed his bride across continents and across the wilds of Africa in search of his dream, and the man who had made her life in its wild and hostile environment, fulfilled and complete.

Because he had travelled the world and had a vast supply of wonderful stories, he had developed a philosophy that was in many ways ahead of his time. He believed that in centuries to come, there would eventually be neither white nor black people on the earth: everyone would be the same colour, and the colour bar in South Africa would disappear as inter-racial marriage became more accepted. I had known only black people and white people and did not understand this at all.

Sometimes we would just sit quietly and listen to the different noises, calls and cries of the veld. Cicadas shrilled, owls hooted incessantly and the nightjar offered its nightly repetitive prayer of "Good Lord, deliverrr us; Good Lord, deliverrr us" from the thorn-bushes. I loved to listen to the bullfrogs down by the river where hundreds of them croaked for hours. They created a powerful symphony which grew steadily to a crescendo, as one by one the full frog orchestra joined in, ranging from the deepest bass of the big, brown bullfrogs to the highest treble of the little green tree frogs. The croaking died down at the end of one recital, but when they had renewed their enthusiasm, the bullfrogs began all over again and the orchestra played long into the night.

Safe on our verandah, we listened to the yowling of wild cats, the barking of baboons, and the frightening shrieks of jackals. The hysterical chatter of the hyenas never failed to send shivers up and down my spine and I used to cling on to my mother for comfort.

My mother was very afraid of snakes. They slithered and curled everywhere and lay on the warm sand or stones at night, when the chill winds cooled the air after the day's searing heat. We had to take extra precautions to prevent snakes from crawling into the rondavels and coiling up underneath the beds or indeed anywhere on the floor. Sometimes they even crawled into our clothes in the cupboards and climbed up the uneven walls of the rondavels and into the thatched roof. We used to close all the doors at sunset, put finely-meshed wire netting across the windows, and place extra lamps all round the open verandah and the stone steps leading up to the bedrooms. In spite of all this, some poisonous snakes still managed to wriggle inside and on several occasions my father had to get his rifle and shoot them inside the house.

On summer evenings the smells from some of the shrubs and flowers were almost overpowering. The moonflower with its six-inch-long white trumpets started to bloom when the moon was waxing and threw off a sweet, heady perfume. This scent grew stronger and stronger till the night of the full moon, when the perfume began to fade away until the new moon started to rise.

Every night during the summer, a peculiar ritual took place. At about half past six, swarms of flying ants as we called them, appeared from apparently nowhere. They are big, fat, brown termites about three quarters of an inch in length, with four gossamer wings about an inch and a half long. These ants wriggled out of tiny concealed holes in the ground and immediately flew upwards in confused patterns. Because flying ants are strongly attracted to bright light, they would flutter round the paraffin lamp which we kept burning on the stoep. We used to run round, shutting doors and windows in an attempt at keeping these flying creatures out of the house. About an hour after first appearing, hundreds of flying ants crawled on the ground or on any flat surface and shed all four wings. Without fail at eight o'clock they disappeared completely, leaving only their wings lying all over the ground in a thick, shining carpet. What happened to them, nobody seemed to know, but there was never a sign of a flying ant the next day. We called them the eight o'clock ants as they seemed to vanish at the stroke of eight.

There was invariably something to watch as we sat out on our little stoep. In the evenings we often saw sheet lightning far away, flickering across the flats right up to the horizon. We always hoped that this would bring rain, but it rarely did. My father told us that it was caused by the hot, low air meeting the cooler, higher evening air.

On clear, moonlight nights, the veld was transformed from the dry, sun-baked brown earth to a place of mystical beauty; the mountain, to a magical kingdom. The calls of cattle and donkeys and the barking of the dogs echoed and re-echoed high up on the cliffs of Spitskop. On these sultry nights, too, millions of fireflies with their little flickering, green lights would fly past, like a thousand sparklers waved in the inky night. Aubrey and I caught a few and put them into boxes, but next day we were disappointed to find that they were nothing but plain grey moths without any sparkle.

Once the fireflies had fluttered away and the eight-o'clock ants had completed their sacrificial wing dance, the four of us used to sit and talk about the farm, about England, the rain (or lack of it), religion, astronomy. We were receiving an education that was to stand us in good stead for the rest of our lives.

In the winter months the bush died, only to burst to life again in spring. This was an idyllic time: we were a happy and contented family. Crusoe was always beside us and if any one of the noises sounded nearer, he would growl menacingly, or make a dash over the wall into the bush after the creature he had just seen or heard. When the cool night wind began to blow, we were put to bed while Crusoe slept on a mat outside our door. The soft sound of my parents' chatter about the day's experiences, their worries and fears, mingled with light, easy banter and the chinking of glasses, wafted over the night air. We listened until we were too worn out to try to decipher individual words and fell asleep, tired and happy.

My parents' conversation ended at about nine o'clock, as it became very cool and dark at night and leopards began to roam quite close to the garden wall. My mother and father then put the chairs away, blew out the lamps and went to bed. Owls hooted to one another up in the krantzes, and the leopards, searching for a meal, stalked, growling and grunting about the mountain in an attempt to frighten their prey out of their hiding places.

* * * * *

Several families of baboons lived up the mountain. They often passed our rondavels on their way down to the river or to the wild fruit trees when they were in season.

When we heard the baboons' barking we used to sit on our wall and watch their antics: they were very comical. The baby baboons often came quite close to us, but were immediately grabbed by their parents, who chastised them loudly and gave them a cuff over their heads and a hard nip on their bodies. The babies would scream loudly and then go to sit on a tree stump or a rock and sulk for a while. However, very soon they scampered back to their mothers for a cuddle and a meticulous de-fleaing. Having made amends, the family then began to forage together for food in the thick bush.

At one end near the foothills of Spitskop there was an area where a few wild fruit trees grew – apricots, plums, peaches and figs. The baboons were particularly fond of apricots – in fact they were almost as fond of apricots as were the colonies of wasps that plagued the baboons. Unfortunately, that constituted a problem for the baboons. They were terrified of wasps and would not climb up any tree which housed a wasps' nest. Sometimes they could not decide whether the nests were occupied or not, as these nests, although always conveniently close to the fruit, were often cunningly hidden by fruit and leaves. The baboons overcame this problem with a brilliantly conceived plan – they grabbed any baby baboon which happened to be sitting on its own and flung it up into the tree right beside the nest. The adult baboons then waited patiently for the outcome of this enforced foraging by the baby baboon. If the baby started to pick and eat the fruit quite happily, the whole troop of baboons would scamper over to the tree and climb up it. However if the baby came hurtling down screaming, this meant that it had obviously been stung and so the troop moved on and sat under another tree which they carefully tested again with another infant.

One day Aubrey and I sat watching the baboons playing about just above the house. Some were jumping from rock to rock, others were swinging about in the tree, and the older baboons were busy turning stones over, looking for centipedes and their favourite delicacy - scorpions.

While we sat watching them cavorting, a female baboon came out from behind a clump of bushes nearby. She was clutching a tiny, pink-eared, obviously newborn baboon. She sat quietly on a rock nursing her baby. We watched in fascination as one by one, the other females went over to the mother and baby. Some of them touched the baby with their hands, and some of them seemed to kiss it very gently while the mother sat happily and placidly nursing her newborn. When this little ritual was complete, the whole troop, including the mother and her infant, walked back up the mountain into the thick bush.

We were so touched at the intimacy of this little incident that we were unable to speak for quite a while. We wondered if we had been watching something that had never been observed by any human being. Had this particular troop of baboons developed a unique social ritual associated with the birth of a new member of the group?

We made our way home in silence. We felt privileged to have been witnesses at this ceremony. At the same time, though, we felt slightly ashamed at having intruded on the privacy of this little community.

* * * * *

Aubrey and I often went with Meofi and Mankahpa to follow the honey bird. It was a very strange bird. It hopped about in a bush in order to attract our attention, twittering and flapping its wings in an exaggerated way, but if we got near it, it flew away to the next bush and grew ever more excited and agitated as we followed it. Finally it settled on a thorn tree and called very noisily but did not attempt to fly any further. This meant that there was a tree somewhere nearby where the honey-bees were swarming. The honey bird usually then led us to a very old tree with a thick trunk where bees were busily flying in and out of a hole.

We smoked the bees out in order to stun them and render them harmless, stuck our hands in and pulled out lumps of honeycomb dripping with honey. We ate till we were almost sick, then we scraped out as much as we could manage to carry back home. First of all, though, we had to reward our guide, the honey bird, by impaling a good slice of the honeycomb on one of the branches on which he perched. That way, Mankahpa and Meofi said, he would lead us to honey again another day.

Sometimes we were led to bees that had chosen to create a hive in a hole in the ground, though when we extracted this honey it was very gritty and mixed with grass and earth. Although Aubrey and I couldn't bring ourselves to eat this mixture, Mankahpa and Meofi were not deterred and in it all went into their mouths: sand, grit, earth, grass and bee larvae. They loved the sweet taste and squelchy texture of the creamy stuff oozing down their cheeks. They said the bee larvae were good medicine and "made their blood strong."

* * * * *

Aeroplanes were in their infancy in the 1920s, but once every couple of years, a biplane would pass over the farm. Aubrey, Meofi, Mankahpa and I were alarmed at our first sight of this strange flying thing that roared across the sky. We ran to call my father, who explained what an aeroplane was. We confidently told Meofi and Mankahpa that the noise was made by a powerful machine that could fly and that it was driven by a man sitting inside it. From then on, every time a plane flew overhead, Meofi danced around, waving her arms in the air, and sang to the pilot and his miraculous invention:

Hoh, leh, leh! Hoh, leh, leh!
Fly mosheen, fly mosheen!

95

* * * * *

As we grew older, we ventured a little further each time into the flatland, across the veld that stretched far away beyond the river, to the furthest boundaries of our farm. Aubrey and I loved wandering about exploring the veld, particularly early in the morning just after daybreak. We looked for thick spiders' webs, strung across from bush to bush and made heavy with dew, glistening in the morning sunlight. We used to chase away the huge spider that lurked in the middle of the web then stand about five yards away and run backwards into the centre of the web in order to be catapulted forwards by the springy strands. Whoever was catapulted the furthest was the winner: this was usually Aubrey, as he was so much lighter and thinner than I was. Whenever we had been playing this game, we always arrived home encased in thick, sticky spider's web. This, of course, did not please my mother at all because she had to pull it off our clothes, a task that was not as easy as it seemed because my knickers were often made of white flour-bags and the spiders' webs often became thickly entangled in the calico.

We spent a lot of time exploring the veld and wandering through thick bush and grass which grew about five feet high. There was always something different to see and we had no fear of snakes, reptiles or most wild animals.

On one of our excursions through the bush, I was trailing well behind Aubrey and had come to a bend in the river about one and a half miles from home. I was picking some wild berries that we called "I'di tetwa", when I heard a loud hissing behind me. I turned and saw a leguaan about four feet long thrashing its tail as it approached. I began to run: the leguaan followed and chased me all the way down a steep hill and kept hissing as it ran. Fortunately at the bottom of the hill yet another hill lay ahead of me. As the leguaan's short, fat legs grew tired, it stopped and squatted down on its belly. I was almost certain that leguaans did not bite, but it was nevertheless a very frightening few minutes. I was most afraid of its tail, which Meofi told me could be very dangerous because one lash could knock a child down.

96

One day, Aubrey and I decided to take Meofi and Mankahpa with us to pick some prickly pears across the river on the veld, where the fruit grew in abundance. We had been picking pears for a while and had nearly filled a small basket, when we decided it was time to set off home. On our way back we noticed a large hollow in a thick tree stump, almost on ground level. Meofi peered right in and immediately let out a scream, shouted, "Noga! Noga!" (Snake! Snake!) and ran away. Aubrey threw a little pebble into the hole and out poked the head of a large python which had been curled up inside. We were terrified and ran as fast as we could, dropping all our prickly pears. When we got home, we told my father and he immediately saddled his horse and galloped to the tree stump, with Aubrey riding in front of him to show him the way.

When they reached the stump, there was no sign of the python. To my father's great amazement, when he peered into the hole he saw a cluster of eggs snugly lying in the hollow. It was too dangerous to put his hand down into the nest in case he disturbed a full-grown python. His attention was attracted to a thorn-bush where some finches were fluttering and twittering about in a very agitated way. He crept nearer, peered between the branches of the thorn tree and saw the tell-tale scales of a full-grown python. He took aim and shot it, then went back to the nest to collect the eggs which he put into a sack. He counted thirty-eight small, round, white, soft-shelled eggs, each about the size of a golf ball.

When he got home he snipped one open. Inside was a perfectly formed little python almost ready to hatch. He destroyed all the eggs and buried them. My father commented, "Well, thank goodness, there will be almost forty pythons less on the farm. Their mother has done enough damage to my goats and calves." He measured the adult python and told us she was twenty-one feet long.

The farmhands collected the dead snake, took her home, skinned her and took out some of her entrails which were hung out to dry in the sun, then taken to the local witchdoctor where they were exchanged for medicine. Occasionally, if the prize was highly valued, the witchdoctor would trade the entrails for a spell which he would cast on someone who had done them a grave injustice. The skin was sold to a local craftsman who made it into shoes and handbags.

* * * * *

Although our district was teeming with so many wild animals, wild dogs had not been heard of anywhere near our farm. One morning early we were awakened by the fierce and loud barking of dogs and the bellowing of cattle in a panic on the veld.

Andries's son, Lesiva, came running as fast as he could, shouting, "Baas! Baas! Tshetsha!"

My father quickly saddled his horse, took his rifle and galloped down to the source of all the commotion, about a mile from the house. He wheeled Dandy abruptly to a halt as he quickly scanned the devastation before him. An ugly pack of snarling, barking, wild dogs was savaging the herd of milking cows by jumping up and tearing strips of the flesh off the cows as they tried to flee or use their horns to fight off the dogs. My father raised his rifle and fired at the dogs. Some of them he killed and some he wounded: these he later killed as well. The rest of the pack ran howling off into the bush. Two of his cows were so badly mauled and mutilated that he had to shoot them, too.

He tried to find the rest of the pack but they were nowhere to be seen. The cows that had been killed were soon carved up by the farm workers who carried the meat back to their homes. The dead dogs were left for the jackals, flies and hyenas; the pickings would be cleaned up by the vultures. The pack never returned to our farm.

* * * * *

Nearly every morning, Aubrey and I used to harness Charley and Nellie and set off from home. As we rode along the path, we smelled the dust as it puffed up behind us, and we listened to the veld as it awakened along with the birds, insects and animals. We sometimes cantered up into Spitskop Mountain, or occasionally along the Soutpansberg, or over the flats towards Bristows Koppies, the furthest point on the horizon.

Considering that my mother had led a very sheltered life in England before she arrived in the bushveld, she showed immense courage in allowing us so much freedom to roam over the veld and up the mountain. She trusted us not to do silly things or be compromised in dangerous situations. Spitskop Mountain was always one of our favourite places to explore as there were so many interesting things we could find to do and see. We spent many happy hours watching the monkeys playing in the trees and bushes. They never attempted to come too close to us, although the baboons were more confident. The baboons, though, were also much less friendly; they barked and shouted at us angrily and sat on trees vigorously shaking the branches to show their disapproval as they tried to frighten us away with their squeals, screams and barks. The bigger ones used to rush towards us menacingly, but we would just stand our ground and face them out. They would then stop suddenly and rush back again to the main troop, where they would sit and watch us.

We decided one morning early to climb to the very top of the mountain. Old John packed sandwiches, fruit and lemon juice into one small rucksack, and in another he put some meat, bones and a tin of water for Crusoe. My father made us his speciality – a traditional English cooked breakfast – before we set off.

The going was fairly easy at first, but after we passed the first ravine the climb became very steep. On the way up the mountain we saw bushbuck, steenbuck and waterbuck which started away and left us to continue our journey. We trod warily to avoid disturbing the snakes which slithered over the ground or hung from the branches.

A little later we came upon a group of monkeys swinging and jumping around in the trees and rocks. They set up a tremendous commotion when they saw us, but we ignored them and they soon calmed down and busied themselves with berry-hunting and de-fleaing one another.

We sat down on a rock for a short rest as the going was now very steep and rough. Aubrey stared intently at the ground for a while and said, "Look at that!" I looked in the direction he was pointing and saw a round, flat boulder with the imprint of what appeared to us to be a human footprint. We thought it was very curious, but we had to leave it where it lay, as the boulder was too heavy for us to carry. Instead we decided to memorise the exact location and bring my father up the mountain the next day to see it. We then continued our way up towards the last part of our difficult climb, towards a high rock precipice.

We rested underneath this precipice for a while and had a drink of lemon juice. Crusoe was very thirsty and glad to be able to flop down, too.

We watched the dassies as they scampered about in and out of the crevices while we kept a tight hold on Crusoe to stop him from chasing them into the narrow cracks between the rocks where he would not be able to climb out.

There were several places in this rocky, lonely mountain where sounds would echo away and back, but this spot was our favourite. We shouted to the mountain as loudly as we could, then we listened to the mountain's reply as our voices echoed and re-echoed clearly, each echo becoming fainter till it faded away.

All this commotion was very definitely not appreciated by the baboons that barked and squealed back. We had heard them earlier on in our climb and we had hoped to avoid them, but they must have changed direction and now appeared to be immediately above us.

We climbed onto a boulder to try to see exactly where they were; they immediately spotted us and became very agitated. They jumped up and down on all fours, yelling and screaming and grunting loudly to frighten us off, then started to roll rocks down towards us. We leaped off the overhanging rock we were standing on, dived underneath, beside the dassies' shelters, and crawled as far as we could into the crevices. Rocks and stones continued to crash down just a few feet away from us.

The baboons kept this attack up for about fifteen minutes, before they decided to move away across the mountain towards the wild fruit trees. By now they were no doubt quite satisfied that the rocks they had sent hurtling down had put us out of action.

The final part of our climb was the most difficult. We had to shin up trees in order to reach the sheer grey cliffs, then inch our way up, grabbing on to tree roots and jutting rocks as we went, hauling and pulling ourselves up and crawling along the steep rock face. We also had to help Crusoe over the difficult parts of the climb where he was unable to jump and his legs were too short to scramble up. Eventually we reached the top. All three of us were bruised and had cuts and grazes on our hands, legs and arms and our clothes were dirty and torn.

After such a long climb we were exhausted, hungry and thirsty, so we sat down on a boulder and took out our sandwiches and drinks. We gave Crusoe some water and the bones we had brought for him and he lay gnawing and licking them noisily, thoroughly enjoying his snack. For a while, the only sound was Crusoe's tongue thirstily slopping water out of the bowl. When we had finished our sandwiches and our strength was renewed, we stood up and looked around us. We were amazed to find out the top of Spitskop Mountain was only about five feet wide, and that there was not one tree, bush or blade of grass there, only stones, rocks and shale.

It was a sweltering day. The heat reflecting off the stones and rocky surface of the mountain was unbearable and we could not sit down on the stones till we had emptied our rucksacks and used them as cushions. We put on our green-lined khaki cotton sun hats to protect ourselves from sunstroke as the sun beat mercilessly down on us.

For a while, with our hands clasped round our legs, we sat and rested on the pinnacle of Spitskop. Looking down and across the veld, we marvelled at the wonderful panoramic view spread out far below us. The slumbering, desolate, flat veld shimmered and stretched far away beyond the horizon. The scene was tranquil yet pitiless.

Here and there, remote little tin-roofed farmhouses glinted in the sun. This was a place of great serenity and solitude, where the silence spoke to our very souls, and we were both caught up in its mystic spell. We felt it, lived it and loved it. We were of it.

We watched the faint little curl of smoke from the train moving very slowly, puffing its weary way to the horizon and past Bristow's Koppies across the deserted Springbok flats on its way to Johannesburg. What, we wondered, was it like to ride in a train? And what lay beyond Bristows Koppies? Even travelling to

Louis Trichardt in a donkey wagon or ox-wagon was to us a very long and exciting journey.

Soon the sun began to throw long shadows off the mountain, the fish eagles' cries came wafting up to us from the river and we heard the call of the male guinea-fowl: "Come back, come back," and the females answering: "Chock, chick, chock, chick, chrrr."

It was time for us to start our long journey back home again down the mountain, and we knew we had to hurry before the sun touched the horizon as darkness followed immediately the sun had sunk out of sight. We also knew that was the time when leopards began to hunt after lying in the shade throughout the day.

As the sun was beginning to sink fast, we walked quickly down the side of the mountain. We chose a route where, with the help of a large, gnarled old tree growing out of the cliff face, we could climb most easily over the precipice. Aubrey was thinner and more agile than I was and could manoeuvre the branches more easily. He swung onto the main trunk and climbed down onto the lower rocks. Crusoe followed him, jumping and sliding, and I brought up the rear. I bent over, grabbed a branch and swung onto the central fork of the tree. I put my right foot into the cleft of a branch, but when I tried to lift my foot up, one of my gumboots became firmly wedged in the fork of the tree. The sun was sinking fast and I was very frightened. Aubrey, who thought I was behind him, was quite a long way further down the mountain by now. Crusoe looked round and came back and lay down under the tree. He began to whine. I shouted, "Aubrey, I'm stuck – quickly, come and help me!" Aubrey looked round and when he realized the plight I was in, he came stumbling back up. Crusoe started to growl very softly; his ears pricked up and his nose twitched. He had heard something. We kept still and listened and for a moment, froze with fear when we heard the distinct grinding grunts of a leopard. We both began to pull and push and shove but my boot with my leg wedged in the tree wouldn't budge. In panic and desperation, Aubrey lifted his right foot up and backwards and gave my foot a resounding kick, and then after another terrible struggle we dislodged my foot from the boot. The leopard's grunts were becoming louder. We both fell out of the tree onto the ground, leaving my boot still very firmly wedged in the fork of the tree. From far below we heard my mother's anxious voice calling us and heard her echo repeating the call, but we were too far away to shout back and besides, we didn't want to entice the leopard any nearer.

I cannot remember very much about the rest of the journey down. We were driven by fear as we stumbled and fell, slid and jumped over bush and rocks. After what seemed a never-ending journey, we arrived back home. We were scratched and bruised and our clothes were badly torn. I did not give my bootless leg a thought on the way down, but on reaching home I saw all the cuts, scratches, bruises and thorns in my leg and foot which was by now bleeding and hurting badly. My mother bathed it in disinfectant and applied bandages, and after a bath and supper, Aubrey and I flopped into bed, exhausted.

We never returned to collect my boot, and as far as I know it may still be there, firmly wedged in the fork of the old tree on the cliff where I so hurriedly left it nearly eighty years ago. My father was very interested to hear about the footprint in the stone. He said if he could find it, he would write to an archaeologist in England to ask him for his views about it. We made several attempts to find the stone but we could not remember the exact place we had seen it. Presumably it still today remains somewhere on the slope of Spitskop in the thick scrub bush: a mystery which will probably never be solved, a sight that may never be seen again by man.

* * * * *

Each week throughout the years my mother lived in Africa, a letter arrived from her sister in Stainton in the Lake District in England, giving her all the news from home. Her mother often wrote, too, and my mother always replied with long, newsy letters.

One Tuesday, the lorry brought our postbag as usual, and we carried it up to my father. He opened it and took out a black-edged envelope postmarked Penrith. He told us to call my mother and then go to play outside while he talked to my mother. Later he told us that the envelope had contained a letter from

103

Aunt Clara, my mother's eldest sister, with the news of her mother's death. We felt very sad for my mother. My father sat up late that night talking to her and comforting her. My grandmother had died some weeks earlier: it had taken six weeks for the letter to reach us.

* * * * *

One summer's night as we were all sitting on the verandah, watching the moon rise and the stars getting brighter in the darkening sky, we heard shouting and the sounds of a heavy, covered wagon rolling over the road past our post box. At first we thought it must be a farmer travelling to Louis Trichardt market to trade livestock.

The wagon passed the post box, then we were very surprised to see it turn up the little road to our home. As it approached, we heard laughter, singing and shouting and the wagon came to a halt right in front of our rondavels.

A young man climbed off the wagon. My father went to meet him. The stranger said, in broken English, "Goot evening, Mr Mefyous! Me, my family and friends have just come to welcome you and your family into the district with a surprise party. I'm a cousin of Mrs Chomse and we live the other side of the flats - my name is Koos Terblanche and these are my family and friends." With that, about fifteen men, women and children clambered out of the wagon.

My mother must have felt very shocked, as her weekly baking day was Monday, three days away. However, he quickly reassured her: "Don't you worry, Mrs Mefyous, we've brought everything – a big braai and plenty to eat and drink and we'll do all the cooking and drinks and we've brought a potjiepot too, all cooked."

The younger children and babies were given dummies and bottles and laid down on our beds where they were very soon fast asleep. Meanwhile the adults offloaded stools, chairs and table, food and drink. Soon chops, chicken pieces, steaks and sweet potatoes were sizzling away and sending mouth-watering aromas into the moonlit air. The men opened bottles of home-brewed beer and handed out lemon and orange squash to the women and older children. They covered the table with salads and fruit salads. The potjie-pot, a pot containing stew made with lashings of beer, brandy, sherry and whisky, needed to be reheated; it was balanced on three stones over a fire and was soon bubbling away merrily.

After the meal, the men went back inside the wagon and brought out guitars, a drum, banjo, mouth-organ, a Jew's harp and a reed flute, and started to play Afrikaans "vastrap" polkas. Two couples began dancing on the verandah which was lit by the brilliant moonlight and three paraffin lanterns. They made my parents join in the dancing; my mother, who was a good dancer, soon mastered the vastrap and waltz, but my father was so clumsy that he decided instead to sit and watch. Meanwhile Aubrey and I were having fun playing with the children and of course, Crusoe, who barked and leapt around excitedly.

Eventually at about midnight, they decided it was time to pack up and go home. Very soon the donkeys were inspanned, the babies who were still peacefully asleep were collected by their

Dalemain 1927. Mabel in front of horse; Meofi in light-coloured dress behind horse; Old John standing on the right.

mothers and everyone climbed back into the wagon. We all shook hands and my parents thanked the visitors for coming from such a distance to give them such a wonderful house-warming.

We watched the wagon trundling down the road. We never forgot these people from so far away across the flats. Although we did not see them again, my father occasionally met them at cattle sales in Louis Trichardt.

105

CHAPTER 8
CHRISTMAS TIME AND VISITS

From the end of October each year, when my mother began to make plum puddings and Christmas cakes, the days became ever more exciting.

We used to sit at the end of the kitchen table and watch her add raisins, currants, sultanas and spices into the pudding mixture in the bowl. She wrapped little silver charms in greaseproof paper and stirred them into the mixture. When this was done, we were each allowed to give it a final stir and make a wish. Finally she ladled the pudding into bowls, ready for boiling. The cake mixture was put into the greased and lined cake tins and baked slowly in the oven for several hours. The aroma that wafted from the kitchen was rich, fruity deliciousness. Aubrey and I were allowed to scrape out the bowls and lick the long wooden spoons. The day before Christmas, the turkey was caught, killed, plucked, and hung, ready for the oven on Christmas morning.

On Christmas Eve we sorted out our stockings and pinned them to the bottom of the bedsteads. Our excitement rose steadily as we wondered what Father Christmas would bring us.

Each year at about this time, a few mysterious parcels arrived and disappeared almost immediately. Search as we may, Aubrey and I could never find them. We went to bed very early on Christmas Eve, tired from having been out most of the day gathering branches of a shrub we called "toveh-toveh" which grew all over the farm. The leaves were very dark green with masses of deep red berries which, my mother told us, apparently looked almost identical to red holly in England. These branches were hung between the thatched roof and the top of the walls so that our home looked very festive and pretty.

In December the temperature at midday in the Soutpansberg is often a hundred degrees Fahrenheit or more. On Christmas day we got up not long after dawn, at four o'clock. My mother, knowing that we were awake and very excited to see all the presents, used to bring cups of tea into our bedroom. She sat with my father, drinking tea and smiling as they watched the delight on our faces and heard our shrieks and whoops of excitement as we ripped the wrapping paper off all the presents that Father Christmas had brought us stealthily during the night.

Once we had emptied our pillowcases and stockings, my father and mother went into the kitchen where Old John sat drinking his tea. They gave him presents wrapped up in bright-coloured paper showing fat, jolly Santas, plum puddings and snowmen, Christmas trees and holly. Old John loved the anticipation of Christmas day almost as much as he enjoyed unwrapping his presents, which were usually shirts, trousers and shoes. He was always very pleased, saying over and over again, "Tenk you, Baas and Missi, tenk you velly mahsh, it velly nice, I rike it velly mahsh."

One year my father offloaded from the donkey cart, some very large and very strange-shaped parcels. We were naturally curious, but weren't able to find out any more about them because they were promptly hidden until December 25th. Very early that morning, we woke up to find Father Christmas had come and gone in the night, and left behind him our stockings filled with books, games, a dress for me and a shirt and shorts for Aubrey, as well as a bag of sweets for each of us.

At the foot of our beds stood two gleaming scooters - Aubrey's was blue and mine was red. We had only ever seen pictures of scooters in the "Xmas Toys" catalogue from England, but it had been beyond our wildest dreams for us to own one. My mother and father were almost as excited as we were; Aubrey and I jumped up and down, shouting.

Christmas day was a very busy time for my mother and Old John. There was much to do in the kitchen for the traditional Christmas dinner.

My father began the festivities by preparing a full English breakfast: fried eggs and bacon, sausages, tomato and fried bread. After breakfast my mother and Old John together started stuffing and trussing the turkey, ready for the oven. When that was done, my mother made mince pies and put the plum pudding into a pot of boiling water.

Herbert, Molly and Robin usually came to stay with us over Christmas. We looked forward to their arrival, particularly as they used to bring us a surprise present. Herbert once gave me a tortoiseshell box which I adored. I kept trinkets in it in my room for many years. Molly's choice of present was much more prosaic. She once asked me what I would like for my next Christmas present and I said, "Molly, I'd love to have a real golden egg like the one in the shop in Pietersburg, please." I had been mesmerised by the golden hen that stood proudly in a glass case outside a shop I had seen on a trip to Pietersburg. When you put a penny in its beak, the hen clucked loudly, flapped its wings and laid a golden egg. Inside the egg nestled a little Kewpie doll and some little pink sweets.

That Christmas Eve, I was pent up with anticipation at the thought of my golden egg. We woke early, and I searched my room for Molly's present, which was prettily wrapped in shiny red paper, but even to my untutored eye, it was distinctly un-egg-shaped. With a sense of foreboding, I pulled away the layers of wrapping paper and stared in disbelief at Molly's present – a cross-work tea cosy and some tapestry wool. Tears pricked the back of my eyes, but I had to blink them back both because I was afraid of Molly and because I did not want to appear ungrateful. I merely swallowed and said a small, "Thank you, Molly." However disappointed I might have been then, ironically in later years, embroidery and cross-stitch have become my favourite pastimes. The following year, my father gave me a teddy bear in a patched romper suit. It had such a sad face that I felt desperately sorry for it and spent the rest of the day in floods of tears, unable to tell anyone why I was crying.

The nearest church in Louis Trichardt was too far away for us to attend on Christmas Day. Instead, after breakfast, we sat on the verandah and sang carols.

We normally ate our meals on the back verandah, but on special occasions, we used the dining-room. Old John laid the dining-room table with a cream lace tablecloth and napkins which my father and mother had bought in Madeira on their voyage to South Africa. He then polished up the silver and glassware so that everything sparkled and shone.

When our dinner was ready to be served, Old John and Maria carried the turkey, vegetables, sauces and gravy from the kitchen to the dining-room. My mother and father had a glass of wine with Herbert, Molly and Robin, while Aubrey and I had home-made lemon juice. My father carved the turkey and my mother served the vegetables onto our plates. Old John, Maria and Malivadja were each given a good helping of turkey and vegetables, sauces and gravy which they took back into the kitchen and ate round a small table which my mother laid with a pretty table-cloth, complete with marula-fruit beer in a jug for John and Maria and some lemon or orange juice for Malivadja.

When we had finished our turkey, Aubrey and I carried the plates and vegetable dishes into the kitchen and Old John brought in the brandy sauce and Christmas pudding which he had set aflame. He took a good helping of pudding and sauce for himself and Maria, while Malivadja enjoyed the bright red jelly and custard my mother had made. Old John also liked jelly and he usually had two large helpings after the Christmas pudding.

After dinner was over, my father and mother brought in the cats' and dogs' bowls and dished up plenty of turkey meat and vegetables for each animal. Crusoe helped himself to turkey meat, and spent the rest of the afternoon gnawing contentedly on a big marrowbone.

When everything had been washed up and cleared away, Old John, Maria and Malivadja went back to their hut to sleep off their dinner. My parents retired to their bedroom where they lay on the bed and cooled themselves with fans made of woven grass, while Aubrey and I stretched out on the cement floor in an effort to keep cool.

At four o'clock Old John came to say that tea was ready in the dining-room. We got up and had a cup of tea and a slice of Christmas cake. An hour later, the savage heat of the day had passed and gentle, freshening breezes were beginning to stir the trees as the veld awakened. The screech of the cicadas began to dull and Crusoe came sniffing and prodding us with his nose, to tell us that he was ready for a play.

My father brought our deckchairs out onto the open verandah, lit the paraffin lamps and watched us play with Crusoe. At dusk, we called on Mankahpa and Meofi and took them a piece of cake and some sweets. Then we went back home for a light supper of cold turkey and salad before we all sat on the stoep and watched the stars as we sang carols once more in the African moonlight. My mother used to tell us a Christmas story before we were driven inside by mosquitoes that hummed, hovered and bit wherever they found exposed flesh.

Tired and happy, we climbed into bed under gauze nets and listened to the nightjar high up in the marula tree as it pleaded continually for the Lord's "deliverrrance". We eventually fell asleep to the symphony of the bullfrogs and owls.

* * * * *

We had few visitors at Dalemain. We were too far away from the more populated areas and so anybody who did venture as far as our farm was made to feel very welcome and never left without having had at least a good meal. Occasionally, about once a year, the local policeman, who had a beat of about one hundred miles, rode in at sunset.

He used to sit up with my parents till late at night. He shared all his local news and gossip, which always interested my parents as he was a very reliable source of information. Then, after a long sleep and a good breakfast, he would saddle up and trot off again into the bush to continue his lonely journey.

My father occasionally rode over the Soutpansberg to visit the Cheales family for a few days. Mr Cheales sometimes came to visit us while Mrs Cheales stayed behind to look after their children and their farm where they tried to eke out a living growing tomatoes. An ox wagon from Louis Trichardt once a fortnight transported their produce to the little cafes and grocery shops in the area. Unfortunately, by the time that the tomatoes had reached their destination, the intense heat often rotted them and many boxes had to be thrown away.

Whenever tramps or travellers came to the farm and asked for food and shelter for the night, my parents always invited them in to share our food and took them to the outhouse where they slept for a few nights till they were once again ready for the road.

So many of these people were English, and a few of them were Oxford or Cambridge University graduates. One of them had been an Oxford don, but for some reason, had just abandoned his home and profession and sailed to Africa. He and other travellers like him were the down-shifters of the nineteen-twenties and thirties. Aubrey and I loved to listen to their stories of their experiences and adventures and we were always sorry to see them go. They told us about their homes in England, what it was like to have Christmas in the snow and how they needed thick layers of clothes to keep them warm. Some of them spoke of their children whom they had not seen for many years, and became quite wistful when they said they must be around the same age as Aubrey and me. They told us about snowball fights, about their school days and how difficult it had been for them to settle down to life at university. One of these men told us that during his trek in the North Western Transvaal, lions had killed two of his donkeys and mauled another so badly that he had to leave his wagon unattended in the midst of the bushveld and walk many miles to find a village where he could barter for more donkeys. The area was so remote that he was not afraid that the wagon would be stolen, but he had to take his remaining donkeys with him as he was afraid that the lions or other predators would kill them. We heard my parents discussing these visitors for weeks after they left us. Why had this educated man abandoned a home, wife and family in order to trek through such a merciless land? What had driven that young man to turn his back on his parents, brothers and sisters? I suspect that my father, who had himself on more than one occasion decided to venture abroad in the face of family pressure, felt some sympathy for these wayfarers.

Mr Brenner, a Jewish up-country small trader, was another occasional visitor. He used to come trotting along in his little donkey cart laden with all sorts of merchandise to sell to the people in the district. We ran down to open the gate for him and he always rewarded us each with a little bag of coloured mieliemeel sweets from his shop and a ride up to our rondavels on his cart.

For a long while after his last visit, we heard nothing of Mr Brenner. This seemed strange because he had been calling regularly every few months. My father heard that lions had killed a trader and his donkeys on the road to Alldays, but we were unable to find out if that had been Mr Brenner. Whatever became of him, we were never to know because he did not visit us again.

111

On one of our journeys to Louis Trichardt, my mother took me to watch a lady giving a catering demonstration from an open carriage on the train from Pretoria. Within minutes, and in front of our eyes, she had whipped up several delicious, colourful and dainty confections. I was fascinated, and have ever since then loved cooking.

* * * * *

Every Friday the cattle on the farm were rounded up and put into a large pen where they would be dipped the next day. Aubrey and I had to count them as they stood draining off in the narrow little passage afterwards. One day after the last cow had been released we found that eight were missing. We told my father who began making enquiries about their disappearance. No-one had seen them, and for a while, a mystery surrounded their whereabouts.

Next day Old John told my father that there was a man from the kraal of the local Venda Chief, whose name was Mpephu. The messenger from Mpephu's kraal, about ten miles away on the flats across the river, announced that our cattle had strayed into Mpephu's mielie field and he wanted my father to collect them as soon as possible. There was no road to the Chief's kraal from our house, though there was a footpath used by the women on their way to either the trading store or to the Sand River where they did their washing. My father told him he would come the next day.

It was midsummer and very hot, so we decided to start off early with Andries, all in the donkey cart. My father picked the way slowly, manoeuvring the donkeys round thorn trees, old stumps and ant heaps. My mother put up her sunshade but it did little to allay either the glare or the heat. She began to wish she had stayed at home instead, but we were all anxious to see the chief in order to retrieve our cattle.

After a journey of several miles, one of the chief's scouts approached us and asked very politely what our business was. Andries told him briefly. The scout ran in front of us to guide us along the way, until eventually he asked us to stop while he went to warn the chief that we were coming. Sweltering under the sun's rays, we sat outside in the donkey wagon and waited for him to return and give us the all clear. At last he reappeared and we followed him to the chief's village which comprised a number of round mud huts with grass roofs. These huts were clustered round another, larger, hut in the centre.

We climbed off the cart and walked behind the scout towards the largest hut. Children were playing, dogs were running round and hens and goats were pawing the red dust. The dogs began to bark loudly at us and the children, all naked, came to stare and giggle at us. The women stood in a group, chattering and laughing loudly.

We approached the hut in the centre. The scout knelt down in the doorway and with his hands together in front of his bowed head, said something to the chief who nodded. My father looked at Andries who translated, "The chief say you mus' come in please."

We bowed low to avoid bumping our heads in the doorway. The chief was sitting on a chair that had been fashioned by hammering a few planks together with large nails. He was addressed as "Morena" (Your Highness) or "Kgosi" (King). He motioned my mother and father to sit down on two similar chairs and Aubrey and I sat on buckskin on the mud floor, which was smeared with cattle dung. Andries sat on his haunches with his hands clasped.

I felt very frightened of the chief. He was a big, powerful man, very dark-skinned. On his head he wore a leopard-skin band with teeth and claws attached to it. From the waist up he wore only a necklace made of shells, claws and thin strips of skin. Round his waist he wore a larger strip of leopard skin strung with several jackal tails which were hanging down to his knees. He was wearing strong and comfortable-looking sandals made of sections of an old car tyre cut to the size of his feet, with strips of inner tubing stitched into the soles and fitted over his feet and round his ankles to secure the sandals. He was speaking in Venda and Andries was interpreting to my father. The talking seemed to go on and on and Aubrey and I began to fidget.

Flies buzzed about in droves in the hut. My mother was waving her Olde English Lavender-scented handkerchief backwards and forwards across her face to keep the flies from

113

settling. Mpephu swished them away occasionally with the tuft of a cow's tail on a stick, Andries flicked his hand across his face, and my father used his hat as a fan.

To add to the stuffy atmosphere, in the centre of the hut a three-legged, black pot bubbled away and gave off an unpleasant smell. It was obvious that the meat in the pot was not fresh. Aubrey whispered to me, "What a nasty smell," and I told him crossly to, "Shhh!"

Aubrey and I looked round the hut. At the top of the walls, lizards were wriggling about catching insects, and spiders were busily tying up the flies trapped in their webs. The thatch was almost black with smoke from the fire in the centre of the hut, and the walls were smeared with brown mud. I watched a spider sliding up and down on its silver thread, and an even bigger spider busily spinning a web directly behind my mother. Assegaais, spears and calabashes adorned the walls, and directly behind Mpephu's chair there was a large picture of Queen Victoria nailed onto the mud wall. When my father asked how Mpephu had come to have the picture, he replied that his son had brought the picture wrapped in a blanket, from a little Jewish trading store. He said he had paid a tickey (three pence) for it and he was very proud of it. The edges were curling up a bit and Queen Victoria had dozens of fly marks all over her.

Mpephu told the guard at the door to take my father and Andries to identify the cattle he had put into the kraal. This was soon done and on their return, Mpephu gave the man an order. Immediately a woman entered with a big pot of locally-brewed beer on her head and carrying three calabashes which she placed in front of the chief. Mpephu told her to give a calabash first to my father, which she did, then to the chief, and lastly Andries. She went out and returned with three big, brown, chipped enamel cups of steaming hot cocoa for my mother, Aubrey and me. Aubrey and I didn't mind its being so hot as it was deliciously sweet, but my mother struggled with hers: she didn't like sweet things and, on top of that, the heat of the fire, the heat of the day and the smell of the unsavoury meat, were almost too much for her. Her cheeks were deep pink, but she didn't want to insult the chief by not drinking it – nor indeed did my father, who bravely swallowed the thick, brown, fermenting beer.

114

My father asked him how many wives Mpephu had and he said six and would we like to see them? He promptly clapped and with that they all filed into the hut in order of seniority. The first wife looked old to us and the youngest was just a young girl. He said he'd paid a lot of cattle and goats for them. He asked my father how many wives he had, and when my father replied just one, he said, "She must be very expensive if you couldn't afford any more." My father asked him what he thought she'd cost to buy and he said, "Fifteen cows and twenty goats and two sacks of mielies." We all laughed, and at that my father said we would have to take our leave and drive the cattle home before his wife became too expensive for him to take back with him.

The chief shook our hands and said, "Uldumela," and we drove back in the donkey cart with Andries and the scout who had been lent by Mpephu to help Andries herd the cattle back home.

Every Christmas day after that Mpephu sent two of his wives to us. Each wife carried on her head a large clay pot, full of marula beer – one each for my father and mother. Marula beer was a drink that my mother really enjoyed. When it was fresh, it tasted like strong cider, but if it were left to ferment too long the beer became very potent indeed. It was made from marulas, wild yellow, thick-skinned veld fruit about the size of a plum. The pulp round the big, inner stone ripened and was then softened manually. The marulas were placed into a smooth, hollowed-out tree trunk and two women armed with round-ended poles stood on either side of the trunk and stamped alternately down on the fruit. At the same time they sang rhythmically and harmoniously at the tops of their voices. The outer skin of the marulas softened and split and released the juice which the women poured off into a big, brown clay pot. The women then covered the juice with reeds and left it to ferment for three days.

We always rewarded Mpephu's wives with thick slices of bread and jam and a mug of coffee which they thoroughly enjoyed. Much refreshed, they left for their kraals, each woman balancing on her head half a sackful of mieliemeel for her chief and a can of water to slake her thirst on their long walk home across the burning hot veld.

115

Dad infront of dairy.

CHAPTER 9
EDUCATION

The word "education" began to feature in my parents' conversation, at first casually and then with increasing intensity and seriousness. The implication of this became alarmingly evident to us: our wonderful freedom was drawing to a close.

My mother told us she had sent away for books, pencils and rulers. She was going to turn the dairy into our schoolroom where she would teach us to read, write and master arithmetic. The experience she had had teaching at Stainton School before she married was about to be put to the test. All this, of course, was very alarming news for us.

One Thursday a large, brown paper parcel arrived on the postman's van. Old John brought it to my mother, who said, "Ah, good. These will be the school books, rulers, slates and slate pencils."

My father made schoolroom furniture from wooden packing crates: two small tables and another slightly bigger; three chairs, a blackboard and a book cupboard. We were told that school would begin at eight o'clock sharp on Monday and we were not to be late, and that our school hours would be from eight am till one pm with two short breaks in between. We considered this to be very badly timed because our most exciting adventures happened during those hours. The tables, chairs, blackboard and cupboard were put into place and our schoolroom was ready.

Monday morning came far too quickly. We looked out of the window and saw the hens all still blissfully fast asleep in the trees. I thought how lucky they were to be able to take advantage of their freedom from being chased by us this morning and roost undisturbed in their favourite tree.

Old John brought us an early morning cup of tea. He looked at us and began to laugh to see us both so subdued, quiet and thoroughly miserable, then he looked out of our window and said, "Rook! You hens cawring you."

We had our tea, washed, dressed and went in for breakfast, then watched my mother walk up to the schoolroom. A few minutes later she rang the school bell and Aubrey, Crusoe and I walked into the dairy. My mother's tone was all very serious. She said, "Good morning, children," and we had to say, "Good morning, teacher."

We sat down on our new chairs. Crusoe flopped down on the floor and began to scratch himself. When my mother saw us giggling at him, she said, "No, Crusoe, you must go out," took him by his collar, led him out and shut the bottom half of the stable door. He barked once or twice then slumped noisily down with a loud sigh.

"Teacher" began to write something on the board. While her back was turned Aubrey nudged my arm and with a crooked smile, whispered, "I feel silly, don't you?" I didn't have time to answer before Teacher turned round, but I remember thinking, well, Aubrey, you certainly look silly with your hair parted down the left side and plastered flat down on either side with Vasoline. Normally his hair looked more like an up-turned scrubbing brush.

My mother taught us to write in copperplate style but I found this quite difficult. I was eighteen months younger than Aubrey and I could not manipulate the slate pencils as well as he did. Aubrey's writing looked a little like copperplate, but my letters were so fat they didn't resemble it at all. We started learning to write on slates so I spent a lot of time rubbing out.

At half past nine the bell tinkled. It was thankfully time for our break. Old John came up with a glass of milk and a bun each for us and tea for my mother. We were allowed to leave the room to go to the lavatory.

When we opened the door Crusoe was still lying faithfully waiting for us. He was overjoyed. He woke up, barked and jumped up at us. All too soon we heard the bell ring, summonsing us to continue grappling with copperplate handwriting. Then at five minutes to one we heard my mother say, "Now children, put your books and slates neatly together on the side of your desks, push your chairs under your desks and leave the room. School is over for today: you must be back in your places at eight o'clock tomorrow." We were delighted at the first part of the sentence, but not at the second part. However, "tomorrow" was still a long way away and we were now hungry.

It was a boiling hot day. Every beast and bird sought refuge in whatever shade they could find. We ate our dinner and went to lie down on the bare concrete in the bedroom until the cruellest heat of the day had passed. We then got up and started to plan our late afternoon and evening activities.

This was to be our way of life from now onwards, we realised. It was a very depressing thought because we were missing so many adventures. We had learned from the other children on the farm as much about the animals and the bushveld as we needed to know. We saw no reason for books and slates, pencils and copperplate hand-writing. Meofi and Mankahpa weren't forced to go to school. Andries, Old John and Motorcar had never been to school, yet they weren't any the worse for it. They knew all they needed to know in life without horrible school!

My mother was a good teacher and Aubrey and I progressed very well. He was much quicker at learning new things than I was but I was much neater than he was. Although my mother was very kind to us, she was also very strict. We were on the whole, well behaved, as we had been very sternly forewarned by my father, "Any insubordination whatsoever and there will be a good spanking waiting for you." He was a man of his word!

Towards the end of our first school year, my mother began to feel that the strain of teaching us in the heat and running a home was becoming too great so my father decided it would be better for us to have a tutor.

At the end of the holidays, after the post had been advertised in a Johannesburg paper, we were told by my father, "A new teacher, Mr Hilton Ward, is coming to take over from your mother in school." A few weeks later, my father drove the donkey cart to Louis Trichardt to meet Mr Ward. We were curious to see him. We wondered if he would be very strict – we hoped not.

Hilton Ward duly arrived and was introduced to my mother, Aubrey and me. He was a tall, well-built, good-looking man of about forty, clean-shaven and with brown wavy hair. We summed him up very quickly: he wasn't going to be very strict. For the first few weeks we were on our very best behaviour – but he was not like my mother and didn't make us work very hard. He was always tired or asleep after breaks and we began to misbehave badly, so much so that one day he told my father he just could not control us at all. It was then that my father found out that Hilton Ward had a drinking problem and after a few months, he left the farm.

We felt very smug. That would be the last chapter of our school life and we were delighted at the thought. Little did we know that arrangements were being made for us to attend a school about ten miles away in the foothills of the Soutpansberg range. It was an Afrikaans school with about forty Afrikaans children and two Afrikaans teachers, as Mr Van der Merwe, the headmaster who came one day to discuss our admission into Spitskop School, told my parents. We were introduced to him; he was a tall, dark-haired man with a Hitler moustache, who wore thick, dark-rimmed spectacles. He spoke to us in broken English and really looked and sounded like a man who would stand for no nonsense at all. We knew then that we had burned our boats and all the crying, apologies and pleas for clemency would be to no avail. We were to start attending Spitskop School in January, at the beginning of the school year, just after the long summer holidays.

The next few weeks seemed to fly past, bringing our dreaded first day at school ever nearer. Finally it arrived. My father took us on horseback through the bush along the foothills of Spitskop Mountain. Strapped to the back of the saddles were little suitcases which contained a week's clothing. As it was midsummer, the evening thunderstorms were too vicious and the weather too hot for us to ride to school and back every day so we had to board there.

That first morning we sobbed bitterly when we said goodbye to my mother and Crusoe, who was not allowed to accompany us. He was howling and whining loudly as he strained against the lead, but he was held firmly. Old John also came out and shouted, "Goodoo bye, solly! Velly solly!"

We made our way in single file along the rocky little footpath through the bush and over the foothills of Spitskop. Finally we arrived at the school gates. We waited in our saddles for a few minutes. I saw a crowd of white children laughing and running round and playing ball, but I couldn't understand what they were saying as they were all speaking Afrikaans.

Mr Van der Merwe came down to greet us. My father got off his horse first then very unwillingly, we dismounted, too. My father had a few words with Mr Van der Merwe, took our cases down and handed them to us. He turned to us and kissed us goodbye. "Now be good and I'll come back for you on Friday." We clung to him, crying bitterly and loudly. He silently hugged us then he shook hands with Mr Van der Merwe, swung up into the saddle and rode away, leading our two horses.

We were firmly gripped by Mr Van der Merwe and steered towards the school. As we approached, the children stopped playing and came to stand round in groups, staring and giggling. They were all Afrikaans and could speak no more English than we could Afrikaans.

Mr Van der Merwe introduced us to them and appeared to be telling them in Afrikaans to play with us. He turned and walked sharply into school.

We were very frightened. The children were not at all friendly and obviously were poking fun at us. They had learned about the Boer War from their parents at a time when some hostility was still felt towards the British, whose fathers and grandfathers had fought them. Aubrey and I stood clutching each other. The bell rang and the children all ran in, leaving Aubrey and me alone outside still clinging on to each other. Mr Van der Merwe came out and said in a thick Afrikaans accent, "Aubrey and Nancy, when you hear the bell ring, you must come into the classroom."

We followed him in and looked round the classroom. The children were still all giggling and looking at us. They cupped their hands over their mouths and whispered to each other. I was shown to a desk beside a pretty, fair-haired girl and Aubrey was told to sit beside a boy with close-cropped straw-coloured hair. The boy and girl turned and looked at each other, put their hands over their mouths and giggled, while the whole classroom poked fun at us, calling us what we presumed to be all kinds of nicknames. One of the chants I learned later was, "Nancy se Ma's 'n apie op 'n stok" (Nancy's mother's a monkey on a stick)!

We didn't know what Mr Van der Merwe was saying as he spoke in Afrikaans, so we just copied what was on the board. When the boy and girl sitting beside us saw us trying to look at their reading books to find out what page they were looking at, they lifted them so that we couldn't see.

Whenever the teacher turned his back or went into the next classroom we were both targets for lucky beans, little balls of paper and plasticine which were aimed at us with the end of rulers and pencils, and which hit us with stinging blows on our faces, necks and heads. We were miserable. I started to cry and all the children joined in, pretending to cry. Aubrey came to me and said, "Don't cry, Nancy." The others all mocked him and told Mr Van der Merwe when he came back, that that new English boy had been walking round the classroom, for which Aubrey received a long lecture in broken English.

The bullying and harassment continued for about four weeks. Then one day as we came out of school, a girl called Lena ran into me, knocked me down deliberately and pulled my hair. That was the last straw. Years of climbing mountains and trees, running through the veld and riding horses, pigs and anything else that could be ridden had made me as fit and strong as any boy. I got up, chased Lena and caught her, hit and punched her and

121

pulled her pigtails till she stood crying loudly. To finish off, I gave her a good, hard slap across the face.

We were not subjected to any teasing after that; the children started to play with us and we very soon learned to speak Afrikaans. Aubrey and I both became very fond of the school as we made some good friends; one of Aubrey's was a boy called Douw Breed. We cried bitterly when we left Spitskop School a few years later.

The school was set on the Soutpansberg mountain slopes on the outskirts of Banyan village, and surrounded by thick mountain bush, shrubs and trees. It consisted of one house that was divided into two – one side for the younger children, taught by Miss Ahrens, and the other for the older ones, taught by Mr Van der Merwe. Aubrey and I were both in the older children's class, for eight to twelve-year-olds.

My desk was against the window and looked out onto a tall marula tree which grew right alongside. In the marula fruit season, monkeys played about in the tree, hopping, jumping and swinging about, while at other times they sat about two feet away from the open windows and watched us. At the same time pens, pencils and rubbers started to disappear mysteriously from our desktops. One morning as I was absorbed in writing at my desk, as quick as lightning, a long hairy arm shot out, grabbed my pen and an apple I had saved for my morning break, and swung away up into the top of the tree. One hand held the pen while the other hand fed my apple into a large, wide mouth. After that incident, wire netting was nailed on to all windows, because it was far too hot to keep them closed. The mystery had been solved and everybody stopped blaming everybody else for taking things without permission. The monkeys now came out and sat on the windowsills and looked very disappointed when they couldn't snatch the trinkets they coveted.

During the week, we boarded at the little boarding house, called "Die Koshuis" (The Boarding-School), which was next to the school. I stayed with the girls in one house while Aubrey was in the boys' house. We hated it. At breakfast time both boys and girls went into the dining-room which was in the girls' house. We all sat round three very long trestle tables. Our breakfast consisted of a plateful of mieliemeel porridge, milk and sugar and a thick slice of home-made bread spread with a very thin smear of butter. The other boys and girls all dunked their bread into the plate of porridge and ate both porridge and bread together. They laughed at Aubrey and me because we first finished our porridge then cut up our bread and ate it. We were such a target of ridicule that eventually we decided to eat as they did and dipped our bread into the porridge. Once we did this, the teasing stopped.

We each kept our clothes in our suitcases. One day Mr Van der Merwe came to me and escorted me to my dormitory where four girls shared two double beds while another girl and I had single beds. He asked me to open my suitcase, which I did, and then he asked me to take my belongings out one by one.

Aubrey, Nancy and Lady on the road to Spitskop School.

Under the last bit of clothing there was a lucky packet souvenir, a little blue aluminium model of Westminster Abbey about one and a half inches high. It was not mine and I certainly had not put it there. I had never seen it before but Lena Laaks, the girl whom I had fought earlier, said that she had lost it and I had stolen it.

I was terribly upset to think I was accused of being a thief and cried bitterly. Mr Van der Merwe obviously believed me. He then began to question Lena more closely, and even threatened to punish her severely if she didn't own up. Eventually she burst into tears and said she had put it there to get me into trouble. After this episode my mother and father paid for us to board with an Afrikaans

123

family, Mr and Mrs Moller, and their daughter, Sofie. Another Spitskop pupil, Sannie Malan, also boarded there.

The Mollers lived in the village of Banyan on the foothills of the Soutpansberg mountain range, near the school. They were gentle, kind people and we were quite happy to stay with them for most of the week.

Aubrey and I spent many hours on Monday afternoons, when we felt very homesick, in the Mollers' orchard. We used to climb a tall loquat tree which looked far away, across to the other side of Spitskop. Aubrey used to say, "Let's cry, Nancy," whereupon we both started to cry pitifully till we were called in for our afternoon tea with cake freshly baked in the oven that the Mollers had created out of a large ant-hill.

One afternoon Mrs Moller sent us with some cakes for her friend who lived in Banyan, on the far side of the graveyard. Sannie, Aubrey and I set off on foot and delivered the cakes. Mrs Moller's friend also had a large orchard where we played hide and seek for a few hours. Eventually she called us in and told us to set back to the Mollers' home as it was getting dark. We decided to take a short cut through the graveyard, where several large and gloomy trees shaded the graves. It was getting quite dark and we were nervous. Suddenly Sannie screamed, "I've seen a body rising up out of the grave over there!" Before we could reply, the leaves of the huge fig tree in the centre of the graveyard parted and out flapped a huge owl, screeching wildly. We were very quickly home that evening!

In summer, Nora and Lionel Behrens from the farm on the mountain next to ours often used to park their donkey cart at Dalemain and travel with Aubrey and me to Spitskop School and back. For a while, Andries also rode with us, but eventually my father allowed us to travel alone. On Friday afternoons Nora and Lionel drove back to Dalemain with us, collected their donkeys and cart from our farm and travelled back to their home.

We enjoyed the winter months, because we rode on horseback daily across the mountain to school, with Crusoe right beside us. He always waited patiently, keeping guard of our saddles and bridles till we came out of school, and then he barked, leaping and twisting in the air when he saw us. He ran towards us and jumped up at us, very nearly knocking us over with his clumsy leaps.

Roads in remote regions of the Transvaal in South Africa in the 1920s were little more than paths. The road to Dalemain was no more than a dirt track three feet wide, and comprised red earth and rocks bordered on each side by thick bush, with a strip of grass growing in between the ruts made by the wheel tracks. As we travelled to school on horseback, we often saw buck leaping and pronking, or a porcupine picking its way across the path. Snakes slithered and zigzagged in front of us, and monkeys and baboons leapt across the road. The only sounds were those of the bushveld: the high-pitched shrilling of cicadas, the strident cries of the brilliantly plumed birds, the rustling of the bush and animals' calling to each other. The smells were of bushveld and dust.

One Monday morning at six thirty we started off to school on horseback as usual. After a while, we came to an area about two miles from home in a thick, bushy and rocky part of the pathway. Suddenly both horses started to snort and rear up on their hind legs and would not move further. We tried to spur them on but they flatly refused to move forward, and Crusoe was meanwhile sniffing the air and growling softly. Suddenly the horses both turned tail and began to bolt back towards Dalemain, occasionally turning their heads to cast panic-stricken backward glances.

When we arrived home we told my father about their strange behaviour. My father rode out there later that day, and discovered the remains of a carcass. A leopard had crossed over the path minutes before we got there and its scent would still have been very fresh. Apparently it had caught and killed a bushbuck which it had been eating behind a thick clump of thorn-bushes several yards away, just out of sight. Crusoe and the horses had obviously smelt this. From that day onwards, that particular part of the path was always referred to as "Leopard's Bush".

After this incident we tried to make the leopard an excuse for not going to school. We would ride so far along our path then gallop back home with stories of the leopard. Unfortunately for us, my father soon became suspicious and escorted us himself – but the leopard was mysteriously never around on those occasions.

For some reason, Mr Van der Merwe, who was very kind to me, treated Aubrey very harshly. I used to think it was very unkind and unfair since he was not, in my opinion, naughty enough to deserve such thrashings. Aubrey was by now about ten years old and I was eight.

I was always very upset when Aubrey was punished so severely and I used to cry. The other children saw me crying, put their hands up and said, "Sir, Nancy's crying." Mr Van der Merwe called me up to his desk, put his arm round me and said, "What's the matter, Nancy? Don't cry, little girl, your brother deserved that hiding as he is a very naughty, untidy boy, but you are such a good little girl I would never hit you." But that would not console me at all and I felt very angry with Mr Van der Merwe. I could never understand why he disliked Aubrey so much while at the same time he favoured me.

Often Aubrey was called up to his desk, told to lean over the back of a chair and given six very hard strokes with a quince cane that he had to cut out of a quince tree. If he presented Mr Van der Merwe with a very thin cane, he was sent outside to get a stronger one.

One day after school, Aubrey and I were on our way back to the Mollers' when we came to the little road that led over the mountain to Dalemain. Aubrey, still very sore and tearful after a particularly severe caning that morning, stopped and said, "Nancy, I'm going home, I'm going to run away." I begged him not to because Mr Van der Merwe would give him a bigger whipping than the one he'd had that morning if he ran away, but Aubrey would not listen to me and said he'd go over the mountain alone if I wouldn't go with him. Although he was eighteen months older than I was, Aubrey was much slighter in build than I was; he looked so pathetic and I felt so sorry for him that I decided to go with him in case something terrible happened to him.

The sun was scorching hot as we started our long, rough hike back over the mountain. After walking about an hour, my heels began to feel very sore and then became so painful that we had to rest under a tree. I took my shoes and socks off to examine my heels, which had both blistered badly. My shoes had sand in them and this made things much worse. The blisters had broken; the sand inside my socks had rubbed into the raw skin on my heels which by now were quite black and bleeding and stinging terribly.

After a short rest we continued our journey along the lower part of the mountain. I couldn't get my shoes on again, so had to walk barefoot. The ground and rocks burned my feet so badly that I jumped from clump to clump of dead grass rather than walk on the road. Late that afternoon, after hobbling painfully for several hours, we finally arrived home. Both of us were crying pitifully.

My mother and father were both very shocked to see us as my father had only that morning driven us to school for the week. Aubrey tearfully told them why he had run away and pulled down his trousers to show them his buttocks which were raw and bleeding from the beating he had suffered that morning from Mr Van der Merwe. My parents were horrified and very angry, particularly as Aubrey's only misdemeanour had been handing in very untidy work. My father said that certainly did not warrant such a vicious attack on a small boy.

My mother bathed and bandaged our wounds and we were sent to bed. We lay on our stomachs all night. The following day my father went alone to the school to confront Mr Van der Merwe. He told him that if he ever beat Aubrey again in such a manner, he would report him to the education authorities and to the police. We were off school for a fortnight, I because I couldn't walk, and Aubrey because he couldn't sit down. When we finally returned to school, Mr Van der Merwe treated Aubrey much more fairly and instead of suffering heavy beatings, Aubrey was now punished by having his hands smacked with a ruler.

A year later, one afternoon just before school broke up for the weekend, Mr Van der Merwe announced that he and the junior class teacher, Miss Ahrens, had decided to produce a play to entertain family and friends the night before school broke up for the summer holidays. He and Miss Ahrens would decide over the weekend who to cast in the play, Snow White And The Seven Dwarves. The parts on offer were a handsome prince, Snow White, an angel, seven dwarves, six fairies and a wicked witch. We

127

were all terribly excited and each girl imagined how pretty she would be as a fairy.

Aubrey and I ran down to my father who was waiting at the gate to take us home in the donkey cart, to tell him this exciting news. Aubrey and I had never heard of, let alone taken part in, a play, although we had several books about fairies, dwarves, princes and princesses and the story of Snow White and the Seven Dwarves happened to be one of our favourites.

I had always dearly wanted to be a fairy, ever since I had heard about them in the stories my mother had read to us. I could think of nothing else all weekend, or for the rest of the week, till Friday. I knew that I, above everyone else, would be chosen as a fairy because I was always well-behaved in class and both teachers liked me.

After our midday break, we all went into our classroom to hear our names called out. Aubrey's name was the first to be read out: he was to be the Handsome Prince; then the seven dwarves, each boy in turn seeming quite pleased. The next was the Angel, the tallest girl in the class, then Lucia van Biljon, my best friend, who was to be Snow White. She was delighted. The girl who was chosen to be the witch was Lettie Badenhorst. I thought she was very well cast. She was a tall, thin, dark-haired girl and we'd never been very friendly.

Next came the six fairies. I was so excited that I could hardly sit still. Mr Van der Merwe began to read out the names of the fairies: Anna! Susanna! Maria! Johanna! Lena! And Hester! the sixth fairy!"

I listened in horror. My name had not been called out. There must have been some mistake, surely? Then Mr Van der Merwe said, "I'm sorry you can't all be in the play, but the girls we've chosen as fairies are fair-haired and blue-eyed, and all real fairies have long, fair hair and blue eyes. Anyway, don't be disappointed because next year we will put on another play, and all those who were not chosen this time will, I'm sure, be in it next time. Have a nice time. School dismissed!"

I could not contain my disappointment any longer. Tears streamed down my face as we approached my father who was waiting at the gate for us.

He looked very concerned when he saw me, and asked me why I was crying. I could not bring myself to tell him, but Aubrey said proudly, if insensitively, "She hasn't been chosen to be a fairy, but *I've* been chosen to be the handsome prince." My father put his arm round me and said, "Never mind, you might be able to help with the scenery or the refreshments or something else." That brought fresh tears. I didn't want to help with either the scenery or the refreshments – I just wanted to be a fairy.

The whole weekend I was very miserable. All I could think of was not having been chosen.

On Monday morning we were taken to school on horseback, but I was still very sad and tearful. I envied the six fairies so badly. The fairies, meanwhile, were so delighted to have been chosen that they formed a gang, played together all week, whispered to each other, and to make matters worse, wouldn't let anyone who wasn't a fairy into their gang.

I remained unhappy all that week, until on Friday afternoon, Mr Van der Merwe called me in to his office and said, "Nancy, are you really very sad because you weren't chosen to be a fairy?" I said, "Yes, sir," and began to sob. Then he said, "Well, now, stop crying, because Miss Ahrens and I have both decided to choose you as a seventh fairy - would you like that?"

I was so thrilled that I started to cry again. I said, "Oh, yes, I'd love it, please sir, thank you very, very much," whereupon he went back into the classroom and announced that I was going to be the seventh fairy.

From then on we rehearsed early every evening, with the fairies and the dwarves learning their songs together. We loved rehearsing because the little songs were so pretty. A Banyan farmer's wife made the fairy wings, while other mothers made the fairies' dresses and the dwarves' costumes which consisted of cotton-wool beards, greenish-yellow jackets, pointed hats and shoes with upturned toes. The Angel had a long, flowing white dress and the biggest wings of all, while Snow White looked angelic in a pink dress with puff sleeves.

Aubrey, the Prince, wore my father's dark suit. Nobody minded that both the jacket and trousers were too big for him despite the fact that my mother had tacked up the sleeves, the trouser legs and the back of the jacket. My father pinned onto the left side of the jacket his First World War medals and two others he had been awarded for bravery against the enemy during the Boer War!

After we had rehearsed for several weeks, finally the night of the play arrived. It was a very busy time for everyone. We held the corners of the tarpaulin, we helped to sweep the dusty ground, we carried water in buckets and watering cans. These would be used to dampen down the dusty ground where the visitors were going to sit under the tarpaulin. We took out chairs and stools and laid the trestle table outside for refreshments. Our mothers made mouth-watering cakes, buns, biscuits, pies, sandwiches and barbecued chicken, boerewors, steak, chops, baked potatoes, pumpkin and salads of every kind, as well as several different tarts and puddings. A big urn with water for making coffee was placed on a wood fire and my mother and some of the other mothers made gallons of lemon and orange juice for the children. Eventually we were all called in to put on our costumes. We were by now really excited.

It was a gloriously African summer night. The moon was up and shone brilliant hot orange, the stars twinkled like fairy lights in the warm, balmy sky. We fairies all put on our white dresses with silver tinsel pinned securely all round the hems and white wings studded with shining silver stars. We wore silver tiaras made of tinsel and silver paper. Everyone was barefoot. Two of the mothers rubbed our cheeks with lipstick, then powdered our faces and painted rosebud lips on us all. We were delighted with ourselves.

I looked at the six original fairies. Powdered and lipsticked, they looked so pretty, just like the fairies in my storybooks. They all had long, fair hair which fell in ringlets over their shoulders, very blue eyes and dainty, lightly-tanned little bodies.

I, the seventh fairy, was a strong, plump little girl with dark hazel eyes and almost black hair with a fringe, cut straight round from the bottom of one ear to the other. I was so excited I did not notice the contrast between us. All that mattered was that I was a fairy.

At last the music started and we stood in line, ready to go onto the stage. We had been told to step down lightly from the classroom door onto the stage, then dance daintily round the little fire burning in the centre of the stage, while we sang a song about fairies. When all six had tripped noiselessly one by one out of the door onto the stage, it was time for me, the seventh fairy, to appear. I hopped out with a thud onto the wooden stage. This brought forth loud laughter and cheers from the audience. A little boy in the second row shouted out, "Kyk daardie swart feetjie!" (Look at that black-haired fairy!); undaunted I hopped around behind the sixth fairy, and it never occurred at all to me that they thought me a comical fairy. I thought they were laughing with me because they liked my performance.

The show continued to great acclaim from the enthusiastic audience until the finale when the Prince, resplendent with his rows of medals, woke Snow White up with a grudging kiss. A donkey was led from a side entrance onto the stage towards the Prince and Snow White, to carry them off into the moonlight. Aubrey got up onto the donkey's back and Snow White was lifted up beside him. The donkey had obviously forgotten its cue because it promptly lifted its head, opened its mouth and brayed loudly. The visitors joined in the pandemonium with loud laughter and clapping.

The donkey, startled by the extra load and the sudden applause, turned tail and bolted off the stage as fast as it could with the Prince and Snow White waving to the audience as they left hurriedly, trying to stay on the saddle of the fast fleeing donkey.

The curtain was drawn across the stage, and we all gathered backstage, ready for our curtain call. When the curtain jerked back, thunderous clapping, shouting and whistling continued for five minutes. Mr Van der Merwe made a speech. My father climbed onto the stage and congratulated the teachers and all the children on an excellent performance and a most enjoyable evening. He handed to Mr Van der Merwe a five pound note to be spent on a picnic or some other outing for the pupils, and we all then went out into the brilliant, warm moonlit night to enjoy the refreshments.

After we had all had enough to eat and drink, my father, mother, Aubrey and I drove home six miles in our donkey

cart. Nobody could have been as deliriously happy as I was at
having been a real live fairy that night.

* * * * *

We both boarded with the Mollers until sadly, Mr
Moller died. After that Aubrey went to Jeppe High School in
Johannesburg, and I went to board with another Afrikaans family,
Mr and Mrs Nothling in Banyan village, quite near the school. I
was very happy there. The Nothlings had a daughter called Mona,
and although she was much older than I was, probably about
eighteen, we got along very well together. The Nothlings loved
entertaining and often in the evenings they invited all the villagers
in Banyan to a party at their home.

These parties were always great fun, but never more so
than on Pancake Evening. Mrs Nothling and Mona prepared
several gallons of pancake batter early in the day and spent the rest
of the day baking all kinds of delicious cakes and little savouries.
The gardeners picked dozens of lemons and squeezed out enough
juice to fill several jugs. Mrs Nothling made a thick lemon syrup
for pouring over the pancakes.

The guests arrived in the early evening in their donkey
carts or on foot. The women, strong and sun-tanned with their
hair scraped back into a bun, arrived on the arms of their
husbands, tall rangy men who walked with the unselfconscious
ease of movement of men who had spent their lives in the
freedom of the bushveld. They brought with them their frying
pans and while the men smoked their pipes and drank coffee on
the wide open verandah, the women tossed pancakes in the
kitchen. We children had great fun trying to toss our pancakes
and shrieked with laughter when they flopped onto the floor.
Afterwards everyone, young and old, played parlour games: beetle
drive, bagatelle, pinning the tail on the donkey, musical chairs,
pass the parcel and many other games. They were wonderful
parties. The guests all left at about eleven o'clock when I was sent
to bed, tired but happy.

At the age of twelve I left Spitskop School to continue
my education at the local secondary school, Happy Rest School,
an agricultural school for boys and girls, run by the headmaster,

Mr Van Wyk. In the mornings the boys learned about market gardening, aspects of farming and animal husbandry, while the girls were taught cooking, sewing and knitting. Afternoons were devoted to academic subjects.

Happy Rest School was situated on the Soutpansberg mountain range on a large site with a huge old colonial house in the centre. This comprised a kitchen, a dining hall for the pupils and a cookery and domestic science room for the girls. Tall blue-gum trees lined the road leading up to the school and continued right round the perimeter of the school. Behind the dormitory was a high, cone-shaped koppie where large rocks jutted straight up out of the ground. Growing amongst the rocks were bushes, trees and stubble grass which was surrounded by thick wire netting and which was always green because it was watered by a spring half way up the koppie. We often saw small buck, including duiker, klipspringer and steenbok, and dassies, on this koppie. They were all very timid and mainly hid in the thick bush, though they could sometimes be seen jumping and roaming about on the rocks with their young.

My window in the schoolroom looked down on the little koppie and I often got into trouble for not paying attention, because I found the buck and dassies much more interesting to watch than the teacher at the blackboard. I can clearly hear the sharp words, "Nency, aandag asseblief!" (Nancy, attention please!)

On Saturday nights the pupils who were learning musical instruments played traditional Afrikaans "opskud" music loudly on concertina, accordion, flute and drums while couples tripped happily round the floor.

On Sunday mornings after breakfast at seven o'clock, we attended a Dutch Reformed Church service in the dining hall. This service was usually conducted by a lay preacher or sometimes by our Religious Education teacher. After the service, the whole school used to go for a picnic about a mile up on the Soutpansberg Mountain. The teachers had discovered a perfect site for a picnic, right beside a little cascading waterfall fed by the spring further up the mountain. The water was crystal clear and cool and we used to enjoy climbing over the rocks and paddling in the little pools. I loved sitting on a big, sun-warmed rock and looking out at the panoramic view of the open flat, empty veld down below.

One hot, clear morning we had all arrived at the waterfall and begun the preparations for the picnic. The braaivleis fire had been lit earlier and the embers were glowing brightly, ready to cook the meat. Sausages, steak, mutton chops and chicken pieces were all arranged neatly on the large grill and the aroma and smoke wafted up towards the mountain. Onions and potatoes, wrapped in banana leaves, were slowly baking in the red embers of another fire. Vegetable and fruit salads, together with stacks of tin plates, forks and spoons, were spread over stone slabs. Jugs of cream and cans of freshly squeezed orange and lemon juice were set in the shade of a bush. When everything was cooked, we each in turn, our mouths watering, took a plate, fork and spoon to the teachers who served us a portion of meat. We then helped ourselves to potato, onion and salad, and lastly to fruit salad and cream and chose a place to sit and enjoy our food.

The three classroom assistants who had carried all the food for the barbecue were sitting a few yards away from us. We were about half-way through our barbecue when one of them came running towards us and with a look of terror on his face, shouted to Mr Van Wyk, the headmaster, "Baas, baas, quick! We must go now! Me and William and Jack, we see a very big leopard very close, he looking at everybody and he growling, he very cross; we very flitting." (frightened).

The teachers told us all to wrap our food up quickly, put the plates, spoons, forks and mugs into a big basket and keep close together. When all the food had been collected into another basket the teachers and assistants quenched the fires with water from the waterfall. We were ushered quickly down the mountain to the school and to safety. In the hall, the food was rescued from the baskets and laid out on the dining hall table, and we were told to help ourselves, although very few of us felt hungry after such close contact with the leopard. We never again went up to the mountain to our favourite picnic area. At assembly the next morning, Mr Van Wyk told us that although it was known that there were many leopards up in the mountain, it was unusual for them to venture down so far. They must have been hungry and smelt our meat grilling. It was too great a risk to hold another

134

picnic on the mountain again, so after this, all our picnics were held under the tall blue-gum trees close to the school. We were very sorry as we loved the picnic place with the waterfall up in the mountain.

My early teenage years were as much an age of innocence as my Spitskop School years, and teenage romance was virtually unheard of amongst children under sixteen years old. Aubrey and I were very friendly with George Bell, as he was the only English boy living near us. All the other children at school used to tease me and say George was my boyfriend, because he sometimes used to let me have a taste of his tin of Nestle's condensed milk which he brought from his father's shop.

One of the bigger boys, Johan Biermann, who lived up on the Soutpansberg, also had a crush on me, but I really did not like him. One day after school he tried to kiss me and I slapped his face. He was very angry and said in Afrikaans, "You like Yors Bell, I know, and it's no wonder, he's so ugly – soort soek soort." (Birds of a feather flock together). This, of course, warranted another good slap from me.

CHAPTER 10
THE RIVER

As there were stories circulating locally about gold mining in the Northern Transvaal, Aubrey thought it would be a good idea for the two of us, Mankahpa and Meofi, to try our luck at prospecting.

One morning we started off armed with picks, shovels, spades and buckets. We were heading for a flat area near a spring up the mountain, about a quarter of a mile from our house. It was a quiet, deserted, peaceful part of the farm that somehow had an aura of mystery. We selected our site and started excavating. Crusoe joined in enthusiastically and began to dig a hole. Aubrey and Mankahpa mainly used the picks and Meofi and I did most of the shovelling. We decided we would all have equal shares of any gold we found. We were digging and shovelling patches of roughly two feet square.

About eighteen inches down, Aubrey held up a large, straight object. He said, "Huh, I've found a bone – look!" We all went to examine it and decided it was a bone from a large animal – probably a bushbuck or waterbuck.

Mankahpa then unearthed a few rib bones and another, larger one. The heap of bones was growing bigger. All of a sudden Meofi screamed loudly. She turned round and fled screaming back to the house, shouting, "Spooks! Spooks!" She was followed in hot pursuit by Mankahpa.

Aubrey and I were surprised by their odd behaviour and stopped our excavation. We looked round, thinking they had seen a baboon or worse still, a leopard, but we heard and saw nothing and Crusoe was still digging away as hard as he could. We continued to dig and shovel, determined to find the gold that would be ours to keep.

As Mankahpa had gone, I decided to continue excavating his hole. I walked across and lifted my pick up to bring it down into the hole. To my horror, I found I was looking down on four human skulls with eight empty eye sockets pathetically looking up at me. I shouted, "Aubrey, quick! Come away, there are skeletons!" Aubrey threw his pick down and we both ran home.

When we arrived at the house, my mother said, "Are you all right? You both look as though you've seen a ghost - you're as white as sheets." We told her and my father who invited Andries to come to see where we'd found the skeletons.

When we arrived at the site, my father looked at the shallow graves. He asked Andries if he knew anything about the skeletons, but Andries answered, "No, baas, but they must be very, very old. I see their spears and pots that are buried with them are not like ours and their bones are very grey and soft so they are very old."

My father could only guess that many hundreds of years ago this site had been inhabited by a long-forgotten people who had been ravaged by either disease or war and had left little trace of their settlement. Some of their bones had been buried in very shallow graves, while others had been left for wild animals to devour. With the passage of time, the remains had been covered with soil and with the thick undergrowth that had quickly encroached on the lonely burial site. We put back in their shallow graves, all the bones, shards of clay pottery, beads and shells, sharpened stones and spearheads which we had unearthed. We covered them with sand and left them to continue to sleep in peace.

My father was thoughtful. We wondered if there were any connection with the footprint we had discovered in the flat stone higher up the mountain and he answered, "Maybe – who knows what the history of this place is?"

Throughout the winter months, March to August, we had no rain at all. The veld died and trees were brown and bare. It was very cold from five o'clock in the evening till ten o'clock in the morning. Often there would be a hoar frost and the shallow water in the troughs had a thin covering of ice. But when the sun rose, the ice and frost soon melted away, leaving a crystal clear, blue sky above a bright landscape.

The spring and summer months, September to February, were supposed to be our rainy season but usually it rained heavily only during a thunderstorm.

We used to have our tea on the open verandah once the worst heat of the day had passed. Every afternoon we scanned the horizon in the west for any sign of a cloud, which could forewarn of a storm and more importantly, rain. Night after night we went to bed disappointed after seeing a little white fleecy cloud appear over the horizon, only to quickly disintegrate and disappear in the hot, dry air.

One afternoon we saw a tiny cloud low down on the horizon. My mother had spent some time listening to the weather lore of the farmers in the Lake District and she had been taught how to detect and interpret small changes in the weather and in the patterns of animal behaviour. As a result of this, she was a very accurate weather forecaster. This time she was convinced that there would be a storm. My father agreed and told all the farmhands to clean out the drains, rake out the debris in the furrows, cover the mielie sacks and secure the blades of the windmill.

The cattle, sensing a heavy storm, had started to make their way up into the mountain for shelter, while the horses cantered up and down in anticipation of the storm. Frogs croaked and crickets chirped loudly.

Aubrey, Crusoe and I were very excited. We gathered in our scooters, balls and bats and closed all the windows. Meanwhile a wind had risen and blew in strong gusts, sweeping up dust, leaves, twigs and anything else lying around. The sky grew increasingly darker till the sun was blotted out completely. There was a rumble of thunder followed by a flash of lightning. We took all the dogs and cats into the bedroom: most of them, sensing the storm, had already hidden themselves underneath the beds.

My mother, who was terrified of lightning, pulled Aubrey and me into the bedroom. She was tense and annoyed because my father was still outside watching the storm's progress. She called, "Come in, Stuart, for goodness' sake, please!" He reluctantly ambled in and sat with Aubrey on the edge of the bed where my mother and I were lying side by side and covering our heads over with pillows. To this day I have an abiding fear of thunder and lightning which, as much as anything, arises from a story my father told us. Once, during a very severe electric storm, he was standing in the front door at Munnik, legs apart, when a small fireball shot right between his legs and went straight through the house, through the back door and outside, where it set a bush alight.

By now the wind had died down, the birds had stopped singing and the frogs and crickets had become silent. There was a dreadful stillness. Then the storm broke and vented its full fury on us. The excitement we felt while the storm was brewing changed to fear when it broke. Big drops of rain started to plop down onto the dry, red earth; rain poured out of the sky while thunder crashed and silver lightning flashed brilliantly, illuminating Spitskop. Rain water soon ran in rivulets down the mountain and bowled over empty tin cans which went rolling, rattling and tumbling over and over as they were swept away.

We sat in the rondavel. It was so dark that we could barely see each other so we waited in silence as the storm flashed and crashed right overhead. My mother and father were always afraid that lightning would set the thatched roofs alight.

About half an hour later the thunder quietened and the lightning lost some of its brilliance. We heard a frog begin to croak. We welcomed that noise because it was a clear sign that the worst of the storm had passed. Soon more frogs joined in and the birds and crickets began their chorus. My mother and I poked our heads out from under the pillows and my father opened the door and went out with Crusoe and Aubrey. The cats were still hiding under the beds because although the main part of the storm had passed, thunder was still rolling round the heavens with a flicker of lightning now and again.

Aubrey and I ran out in our bare feet. We were very excited and jumped and splashed about in the puddles and mud. The cattle started to leave the shelter of the mountain and chased and poked each other, or met each other in mock battle on their way down to the flats.

Crusoe bounded about, chasing frogs which popped up all over the place, and leapt up trying to catch locusts and grasshoppers. The black clouds rolled away towards the eastern horizon, leaving behind them the sun shining brightly in a clear, blue sky again. Everything looked and smelled as if it had been washed clean.

My father walked all round to check for any signs of storm damage and repaired whatever he could. The cats came out from under the beds, first sniffing the air at the doorway in order to be fully satisfied that all danger had passed. They then carefully and gingerly picked their way over the wet ground and sat in the sun on the stone wall where they began to clean themselves.

* * * * *

The river which ran through the farm was named the Hout (Wood) River, because of the big mimosa thorn trees that grew all along the banks that twisted and uncurled before the Hout spilled into the Sand River seven miles downstream from Dalemain.

We loved the river and spent many happy hours playing in the water and on the riverbank. For most of the winter months the thin little rivulets of water from the storms were not strong enough to set the river flowing, and just trickled into muddy pools which were havens for reptiles.

Aubrey and I used to jump in and out of the pools and had great fun trying to catch the many long-whiskered barbel that had become trapped and were lashing about furiously in the evaporating pools. We once did catch a few and took them home, but my mother said they weren't real fish since they had no scales and she generally didn't like the look of them. We tried eating them but they were very bony and had an unpleasant, muddy taste so they were cut up and given to the cats who thoroughly enjoyed them.

Fish eagles stood by the side of the pools and caught the barbel, some of which they ate on the spot and some of which they took home to their chicks. Fish eagles are magnificently big, powerful birds. They were known as the Lords of the Skies and their distinctive cry, which could be heard from afar, was the cry of Africa. I loved to listen to this loud, lonely, repetitive call which echoed through the bush as they threw their heads back in defiance. Sometimes we would watch them land on the river bank and sometimes we would watch them fly towards a pool, swoop low over the surface of the water and with their sharp talons,

140

scoop up a fish, fly away and settle on a branch where their strong beaks would tear the fish apart.

The morning after a storm, when the fish eagles were not swooping over the river, baboons and monkeys used to quench their thirst and then play for hours in the mimosa trees along the banks.

In summer, the rains were a little more frequent and the river was at least able to flow gently. In full flow, Hout River was about twenty feet wide. However, when the current was not too strong, Meofi, Mankahpa, Aubrey and I sometimes used to swim and play in it all day. We were not afraid of the water snakes that went gliding back and forth just under the surface and caught beetles and insects that were skimming about. Although water snakes are apparently very poisonous, they seemed to take no exception to us and never harmed us.

Crusoe loved the river and jumped in and out after us, swimming right beside us all the time. We had to hold on very tightly to him as buck came down from the mountain to drink, and we were afraid that their sharp little horns would gore him if he chased them and attacked them.

However, this quiet, peaceful river showed its darker side after a heavy thunderstorm and cloud-burst. Our friendly river became an angry, cruel, swiftly-flowing and raging giant, mercilessly sweeping off anything in its way, then burst its banks and widened to a torrent of up to a hundred and fifty feet.

We were fortunately never caught up in any of these floods but we enjoyed running down to watch the frightening force of the water. We often saw animals, trees, thatched roofs, blankets and parts of huts swirling by in the raging torrent.

Once as we stood watching one of these flash floods, Aubrey noticed a large object being swept along on the floodwater. For a while we could not make out what it was, but eventually the object took on the shape of a woman who was being tossed and turned about by the force of the water midstream. With one arm she held a little bundle as high as she could above the water and tried desperately but unsuccessfully to grab onto any branch, tree stump, root or indeed anything at all that was swirling past her. We heard her frantic shouts for help

141

above the roar of the flood. It was useless trying to wade out towards her, as the water was too deep and the current too strong.

My father jumped onto his horse. Fortunately he usually had a long rope hooked onto his cowboy saddle. He cantered along the riverbank, where he hoped he would be able to lasso her and haul her to safety. However, the bush which grew thickly on either side of the river slowed him down. Eventually he spotted her about a mile downstream where she had been caught up on the branches of an old tree stump. He managed to throw the rope round her body and pull her out of the water, but too late – she was dead. On a branch further down-river he spotted the little bundle which she had so bravely tried to save. It was her tiny baby, also dead. Nobody knew where she had come from, or who she was, so she was buried the same day with her baby, close to the bank where she was found. We guessed she must have been trying to cross the river when she was caught by the flood a few miles further upstream.

After the floodwaters had receded, we often used to see all kinds of strange sights such as monkeys, dogs, goats, poles, parts of thatched roofs, buckets and skins that were sometimes strung across overhanging branches.

The carcasses did not stay there long before the vultures spotted them, and as the birds landed on them, very often their heavy weight caused branches to snap off onto the ground. From there the jackals and hyenas took over, leaving only bones for the vultures to pick clean.

* * * * *

One very hot summer's morning, we all set off early to spend the day with some neighbours, Mr and Mrs Smit. Mrs Smit was Mrs Chomse's sister and farmed across the river and about twelve miles away, on the Springbok Flats. My father rode on Dandy, my mother, Aubrey and I went in the donkey cart and Crusoe brought up the rear.

As there had been a drought for many months, there were only shallow pools of water on the riverbed. Although there was no bridge over it, we crossed the sandy bed quite easily in the donkey-cart and with my father on Dandy, we finally arrived at Mr and Mrs Smit's house.

We spent a pleasant day with the Smits and then at about three o'clock in the afternoon, my mother looked towards the western skies and said, "Stuart, I think we'd better be making our way home. It's looking very black over in the west and we don't want to be caught in a flooded river."

My father looked at the sky and said, "Yes, I think you're quite right," and we went to inspan the donkeys. Towards the west, in the direction of the river, the sky was darkening every minute.

When we reached the river we found that it had already begun to flood. The water level was rising quite quickly and twigs, leaves and grass flowed past. My father decided to take us in two groups across the river to the other side. My mother mounted Dandy behind him, and they rode safely across, then he returned to collect Aubrey and me together. He left the donkeys and cart with Crusoe sitting on the driver's seat, on the other side, and waded back for the cart and donkeys. The donkeys were becoming nervous as they were by now standing knee deep in water, as the river was rapidly becoming broader and stronger.

He reached the donkey cart and started to drive it across the river, which was by now flowing fast and strong. When they came to the middle of the river, a sheet of water caught them broadside on and swept donkeys, cart, my father and Crusoe round and round, downstream. The donkeys began to panic as they swirled downriver, with my father unable to stop them. Suddenly to our horror, Crusoe jumped off the cart into the water and was quickly swept out of sight.

My mother, Aubrey and I started to panic and shouted to my father as we ran down the thorny banks and tried to keep up with him and the cart, even though by now they were a good distance away.

The donkey-cart was washed about three hundred yards downstream. Suddenly, a huge wave crashed against the back of the cart and forced it and my father towards our side of the bank. The donkeys at last felt solid earth beneath their feet, the cart wheels jolted and my father jumped out of the cart. He held on to the donkeys' harness and waded out ahead of them. He caught

143

hold of their bridles, pulled and urged the exhausted and terrified donkeys onto the bank. For several minutes both donkeys stood panting and gasping for breath on the banks of the river. My mother, Aubrey and I cried with relief. Crusoe, however, was nowhere in view. My father got onto Dandy and rode down the river bank; all the while we feared the worst for Crusoe. Several minutes later my father came back with Crusoe following slowly behind him. Crusoe looked very bedraggled and panted heavily, his tongue hanging several inches below his jaw. We ran to him and patted and hugged him with relief, because we did not think he could possibly have survived in the angry, muddy water.

My father, who was asthmatic and was also by now gasping for breath, stood at the side of the cart. When he eventually got his breath back all he said was, "That was a near one." The donkeys quietened down and stopped shivering and my father led them back up to the road where Dandy was standing quietly cropping the grass.

We settled ourselves in the cart and drove slowly home.

CHAPTER 11
PROGRESS AND PROPHESY

Farmers in the early 1920s in the far Northern Transvaal had much to contend with. The land was rough, wild and hard as sometimes droughts lasted for years. Undaunted, however, my father decided to cultivate four acres of flat land down by the river into a mielie plantation.

He had made the three-day journey to Louis Trichardt with Andries and one of Andries's sons, Lesiva, in order to buy the most up-to-date equipment available: a one-share plough and a harrow.

Before the land could be cultivated, it had to be cleared of boulders, stones, shrubs, trees, bush and thick undergrowth. After many months of hard labour spent clearing the area, the soil was finally ready for the plough. One morning at daybreak, Andries and two farmhands caught and inspanned six oxen. They hoisted up plough, harrow and sacks of mielies onto the wagon and drove it down to the area about to be cultivated. My father and mother, Aubrey, Old John, who was going to cook for us, and

I, followed in the donkey cart. The oxen were unhitched from the wagon, plough, harrow and mielies were lifted down, and finally the oxen were hitched up to the plough.

The oxen had no idea what they were supposed to be doing. However, undaunted, my father picked up the plough, manipulated it into the right position and held on as fast as he could. Mankahpa took the lead rope in front of the oxen, William cracked his long whip and the six oxen jerked away in six different directions. After much shouting, whistling and coaxing, prodding and poking by all the men, the oxen started to get the idea and very unwillingly they began to follow Mankahpa.

To keep the oxen moving was one problem, but to keep them moving in a straight line was another matter altogether. They repeatedly wandered out of line when they decided to snatch a snack of a tasty little bush or tuft of grass, but eventually they zigzagged their way down to the bottom of the land.

Meanwhile my father was struggling against tremendous odds to keep the ploughshare in the rock-hard soil. He pulled and shoved the handles this way and that, all the time cursing under his breath. Immediately behind my father, Andries scattered mielies, a handful at a time, into the newly-turned furrows.

Aubrey's, Crusoe's and my main task was to run backwards and forwards behind the plough and shoo away all the birds, reptiles, monkeys and rodents, which seemed to think that all this hot, hard work was being done especially for their benefit. Despite our valiant efforts, they all scampered off or flew away with hands or beaks full of mielies. Once they reached the opposite end, they settled down and waited patiently for the next scattering. By this stage we had done so much running about that we were exhausted and couldn't chase them any more.

The ploughing had to stop at midday, when the sun became so hot for both man and beast that we all trekked home, weary and exhausted. Next morning at daybreak, we all returned to the flats and continued sowing and ploughing. This pattern of work continued for days till the last furrow had been completed. Here and there were a few solid patches of earth which the plough had not been able to penetrate or which for some reason the oxen had decided to walk round rather than over. On the whole my father was quite satisfied with progress.

For several weeks after that, the sun baked down and the ground grew ever drier; eventually, however, the rains came just in time to save the crop and we rode down every day to see the mielies sprout. That year it rained sufficiently for them to grow and yield a fairly good crop.

The crop would have been much better had the baboons and monkeys not raided the land every day. My father organized some of the farmhands into a security rota to keep the marauders away. These guards walked up and down the land, beating tin cans and whistling and clapping sticks together to make as much noise as possible. Two men walked up one way and two of them walked down the other. However, it was a very wide area to patrol and as soon as the guards moved down to one end, the thieves sneaked into the other end, stole as many cobs as they could, then scampered back into the bush before the patrol could catch up with them.

My father stood in the middle of the mielie crop and fired a few shots into the air. At first it frightened off the vandals, but they soon became used to these loud bangs and took no more notice of them. It was hopeless: they outwitted us every time. They had won.

The following year was easier. There was no need for further land clearance, so enthusiastically my father ploughed again, while Andries scattered mielies and Aubrey, Crusoe and I chased away the birds, reptiles and rodents. We then sat back and waited for rain, but none came and the ground was bone dry. A few little plants dared to poke up above the ground but were very quickly scorched and just perished in the blazing heat of the sun. It was a great disappointment. That year we had several very severe electrical thunderstorms but no rain at all. The Hout River dried up almost completely, and we were all very grateful that we had the windmill which blew mostly at night, and kept us, the farm labourers and the cattle well supplied with water. Some of the bigger buck from the mountain even came down at dawn to sip nervously from the trough. We kept Crusoe and the other farm dogs in a hut to stop them from chasing the buck.

* * * * *

Our only modes of transport were on horseback or in the rattling old donkey cart, both of which were inconvenient, hot and slow. My father had toyed for some time with the idea of buying a car, so that we could all travel together in comfort and with greater speed over long distances.

One day Aubrey and I drove him in the donkey-cart to Mara station to catch the train to Louis Trichardt. My father had an appointment with the General Motors Garage, where he intended to look at different models of cars with a view to buying one.

Two days later while we were playing with Meofi and Mankahpa we heard a soft purring noise, which gradually became louder and louder. We could see dust rising above the bush which hid the road from view. Gradually the purring became a growl, then a roar, when with a loud hoot, my father made his triumphal entrance in our new car. The driver, a young man from the town, steadied the car over the heavily rutted dirt road. We all ran out to see our shiny new mustard-coloured 1931 Chevrolet churning up the driveway and rumbling through the gate and come to a standstill in a cloud of fine, red dust beside the front steps of the house. My father waved gaily to us from the passenger seat. The farmhands stood staring in amazement, then after a bemused silence, animated chatter broke out.

We were very excited. My father jumped down and introduced us to Jan, the young salesman who had driven him from Louis Trichardt, and who was to stay with us for a week in order to teach my father how to drive.

We examined the car inside and out. It had large wheels, each with dozens of spokes and narrow rubber tyres. Aubrey and I gazed at it and kept getting in and out of it and sitting down in the seats. In the afternoon Jan took us all out on the little dirt road to Mara for a drive. It was much more comfortable than the donkey cart. The canvas hood folded back and celluloid windows with aluminium frames slotted into the four doors for protection from rain, wind and dust. Aubrey and I felt very superior when we passed people we knew who were

148

jogging along in their donkey carts, and we waved regally from the back seat.

Later on in the week, after several intensive hours of driving instruction, my father felt confident enough, under Jan's supervision, to drive over to Bells' store for petrol. Aubrey and I climbed into the back seat. My father started the car off noisily; its gears screeched alarmingly, the car back-fired, jumped and jerked till it finally settled down with a contented purr. At Bells' gate my father was told to change into low gear and gradually apply the foot-brake till he came alongside the petrol pump, when he was told to pull up the handbrake.

My father had been a horseman all his life, and for a couple of years in his youth, as a cowboy in the Wild West, he had trained bucking broncos. He was used to having his commands obeyed by his horse instantly and did not understand mechanical instruments at all.

Instead of putting his foot on the brake he started reining in on the steering wheel, pulling it as hard as he possibly could, shouting, "Whoa! Whoa! Whoa, you brute when I tell you!" with his right foot still jammed firmly down on the accelerator.

The car lurched forward, rammed into the tall pump and bent it back. Jan grabbed hold of the handbrake and pulled it up as far as he could so that the car jolted to a halt over the pump. Mr Bell came out, shouting and waving and very angry, his bloated face the colour of beetroot. He eventually calmed down when my father said he would pay for all the damage he had caused.

My father was not a good driver and did not like driving, and was therefore quite agreeable for Aubrey to learn to drive. Aubrey became a careful, steady and reliable driver. He taught me to drive when I was twelve, and for a while, I enjoyed driving the Chevrolet.

One day as we came back from Mara, I was in the driving seat and was inwardly congratulating myself on how well I had driven all the way home. Just before we reached the house, Aubrey said, "Oh, look! There's George Bell in their new car passing by the post box!" I turned my head to look and forgot all about the steering wheel, until I felt a heavy bump and watched

149

the wall that formed the side of six steps up to the verandah, slowly crumple and fall over in a pile of rubble. I was not allowed to drive again, and like my father, found horses much easier to control.

* * * * *

For five years we lived happily in the rondavelo. My father, however, had always intended to build a more comfortable house with a bathroom and separate bedrooms for Aubrey and me, so he drew up some plans which he took to Louis Trichardt where he had an appointment with the building inspector. The plans were approved without any need for alterations because at that time there were very few restrictions on what farmers could build on their farms. Soon the donkey wagon, which was still used to transport heavy equipment, was grinding back and forth, transporting timber, cement, plaster and corrugated metal sheets from Louis Trichardt.

Because it was too expensive to buy and transport from the town such large quantities of ready-made bricks, my father decided to cast his own on the farm.

His first task was to carefully measure out the correct dimensions for the brick moulds. Once he was satisfied with the size, he hammered wood into the shape of a mould for three identical bricks. He selected an area down by the river where there was both good, strong clay and plenty of sand nearby to mix into the mortar.

The mixture was slapped into the mould, levelled off and carried to ground nearby which had been cleared and flattened. The mould was then turned over and lifted off, leaving three new red blocks ready to be dried in the sun.

My father had engaged several men to make the bricks. These workers spent weeks mixing, filling, emptying and drying while the heaps of bricks grew rapidly. When they had dried out, the bricks were stacked up, loaded into the wagon and taken to the kiln where the firing began. The kiln, at the side of the house, was a hollowed-out and disused ant heap several feet high, heated by burning mielie cobs.

The site my father had chosen for our new home was large and open, behind the rondavels that nestled in the foothills of Spitskop. He and Andries marked out the site for the foundations. We watched the builders and listened to them as they lifted their picks high overhead in unison, chanting harmoniously all the while, and ending with a loud, "HUH!" as they brought the picks down into the earth. After a while, the chanting stopped and the builders laid down their spades and picks. Andries went to my father and said, "Baas, they don' wan' to dig here any more."

"Why on earth not?" asked my father in exasperation.

"They find bones, baas, lots of bones. They say the bones belong to their ancestors and if they move them, their ancestors get very angry. They say this not good place for building – it very bad luck to build there, baas. They say no good come if the baas build here."

My father went over to examine the digging. Several skeletons, shards of pottery, spearheads and bracelets were buried or partially exposed below the planned foundation of the new house. My father, who had been disinherited by Canon Mathews and had had a surfeit of religion in his youth, was not a man to tolerate religion or superstition. He became very irritated. "Very well, then," he replied, "we'll move your ancestors. Tell the men to remove the bones and everything else and bury them over there. You can consecrate the ground or do whatever you need to pacify your ancestors – tell them I take full responsibility for moving the bones – but the foundations must stay here."

Andries relayed this to the team of builders. After some discussion and much shaking of heads, clicking of tongues, and cries of "Hau!" the bones were carried over to a new burial site and laid to rest there, then covered with the red earth. A slow, mournful chanting wafted over the early evening air as the builders paid their final respects to their ancestors.

Aubrey and I were not able to witness a lot of the building as we were away at boarding school. Each Friday we arrived home to find the brickwork getting higher and higher, till one day we arrived to discover the brickwork complete and the new corrugated zinc roof flashing in the sun.

151

After only a few more weeks, the house was ready for us to move in. The empty rondavels were very quickly knocked down and the thatched roofs set alight. Dozens of lizards, spiders and grass snakes crawled or slithered out and disappeared into the bush. We felt quite sad to see our rondavels disappear as we had been so very happy living in them. Before long there was no trace of any of them.

We loved our new house and felt very grand. We travelled to Louis Trichardt to buy new dining- and sitting-room furniture and deckchairs for the back and front verandahs, where we would spend many happy hours.

My parents gave a housewarming party for our three closest neighbours: the Chomses, the Bells and the Behrenses. My mother made cakes, sandwiches and puddings and home-made toffee for the children. The ladies sipped a glass of marula beer while the men each downed a couple of bottles of Lion Lager. Later on tea and coffee were served. The grown-ups sat on the verandah chatting contentedly and listening to the crickets, bullfrogs and the animals of the bushveld. We children played games which seemed to be even more exciting than usual under the great, golden African moon. Eventually it was time to leave, and one by one the donkey carts creaked and trundled down the driveway. For better or for worse, a new era had begun at Dalemain.

* * * * *

As I had always been more interested in farming than Aubrey was, my father had a special surprise for me on my tenth birthday.

"Nancy," he said, "if I buy some goats for you, would you like to look after them? You'll have to tend to any sore hooves, ears or udders and make sure the goats are kept safe – would you like to do that?" I was delighted at the prospect of owning my own goats and promised I would look after them.

All that week the farmhands were very busy building a round thorn-bush kraal with a shed at one end where the goats could shelter. In the centre of the kraal was a large, round piece of ground on which grew several small thorn trees and some tall

152

grass, where the goats would be spending most of their time. One evening the following week, a lorry laden with bleating goats arrived.

As I would be away at school, two cousins of Meofi and Mankahpa volunteered to herd the goats and bring them back to the kraal at sunset when the jackals and hyenas began to hunt for food. During the winter months when the grass and leaves were very dry and brown, they shepherded the goats up into the mountain to feed off the greener leaves of the thorn-bushes. I always marvelled at the deftness with which the goats picked their way into the centre of thick clusters of trees with viciously hooked thorns, and gingerly curved their tongues round the branches in order to avoid the thorns and pull off the succulent leaves.

When the little goatherds heard the fish eagles' cries up the mountain, and the guinea-fowls' calling to each other down by the river, they knew it was time to bring the goats back to their kraal, before the leopard began to stir. The little goatherds' repeated calls of, "Hur-oo-wur, hur-oo-wur", always brought the goats down from the mountain.

Meofi, Mankahpa, Aubrey and I often went across the river to join their cousins. We all used to sit under a shady bush and nibble wild fruit and berries.

At about midday we became hungry, and Meofi and Mankahpa opened up a calabash into which they had put a serving of stiff, white mieliemeel porridge. They then caught a nanny goat, tied her back legs together, tethered her to a tree, and directed the sweet, creamy milk straight from her udder into the porridge. They untied the goat, mixed the porridge and milk together, poured some into their cupped left hand and sucked it loudly. When the calabash was empty, they licked their hands clean. Aubrey and I used to pick a wild watermelon, crack it open on a stone, remove the pips and then eat the sweet, watery flesh.

I sometimes had to treat nanny goats suffering from mastitis. My father told me that the treatment for this condition was to apply hot compresses and milk the goat to the last drop. His years studying farm management in England had also prepared him well for the rigours of backveld farm life. Sometimes, too, I had to treat infected hooves or goats with tick or fly bites. I used to pick out the ticks and thorns, clean out the goats' ears and hooves with antiseptic solution and apply a strong disinfectant. Wounds in their hooves were usually caused by treading on the large, double-edged "bok-duwweltjies" or, as they were sometimes known, the "boot protector" thorns. These thorns often penetrated our bare feet, as well, and my mother and father had to pull out sharp spines and syringe the holes they left in our feet.

I loved looking after my goats and tended them diligently, and even on occasion, helped them give birth. Despite all the time I spent with them, I was really frightened of the big-horned billy-goat. He would stare at us for a few seconds then, head bent low, tail up and snorting, he would charge straight at us. Many was the time that I had to climb up a tree in the kraal and cling on to a branch as the old billy-goat butted and crashed his horns against the trunk. Occasionally I was unable to climb the tree, but had to run round it while Billy made a menacing noise behind me, until Aubrey came to my rescue. Billy then immediately started to chase Aubrey and once or twice Billy's horns caught Aubrey and lifted him off his feet. Fortunately someone nearby always managed to distract Billy by driving him off with sticks. Aubrey had much more respect for Billy after each encounter.

Early one hot summer morning I went out to tend to my flock before they were let loose to graze on the veld. When I arrived at the kraal, the gate was wide open and all the goats and their kids were gone. I looked around but there was no sign of them anywhere.

I ran back to the house to tell my father, who immediately went to make enquiries at nearby villages, but the goats seemed to have just vanished. Nobody had seen any stray goats or heard anything about them. The police were informed but even they could find out nothing at all. Someone had obviously taken them silently away during the night and my herd had vanished without trace.

My father was very annoyed and I was very upset as it had been such a special birthday present, and profitable, as well: my fifty goats had in the space of two years, multiplied to sixty.

* * * * *

Our new schools, Jeppe and Happy Rest, were preparing us for life away from the farm. Even though I loved the farm and the mountain, I secretly knew that one day, things would change and that I, too, would have to move far away in order to find work. We were gradually taught to accept more responsibility by learning the skills that were valued in the world away from Dalemain.

For Meofi and Mankahpa, too, there were changes. Meofi told us one day that she, too, would be going to a school near their village where she would be taught how to be a good wife and mother, while Mankahpa had a while ago already learned at his school how to be a husband and head of the household. Meofi was away from the farm for a few days. I was eager to hear how she had enjoyed her school. Meofi, however, stayed inside her home for the next few days. When she eventually emerged, she was pale and very subdued. I asked her what she had done at her new school and if she would be going back. She told me that another woman had cut her and pushed what she called soap up her vagina. Mankahpa had also been cut at his school, though she did not elaborate. I did not understand what she could mean or why these terrible things had to happen at their schools. They told us that neither of them needed to return to school as they had now learned about being grown-up. From then on, our evening games were at an end. My lively and creative little friend, Meofi, who had sung and waved to the flying machine, sculpted beautiful clay models and shrieked with laughter at The Laughing Policeman, became very quiet and spent most of her time with her mother, cooking and cleaning inside their hut.

* * * * *

One hot, summer afternoon I was lying on the cement floor in the bedroom, trying to keep cool. My mother and father were fast asleep on top of the beds, when Aubrey burst into the rooms in a state of high excitement, shouting, "There's a cloud on the horizon! Quick, come and see! Hooray! It's going to rain at last!"

We got up immediately and ran to the door. Sure enough, a long, low, brown cloud was brooding just above the horizon.

My father said, "About time, too, because the crops are beginning to wilt very fast," and immediately he started to organize the farm workers to batten down the mielie sacks and rake out the furrows.

We looked again at the cloud. It was bigger but still the only one visible. The western sky was clear blue and cloudless, except for the ominous, dark cloud which was spreading fairly rapidly, staining the whole sky brown. My father and mother looked at each other. My mother drew in her breath sharply and clutched my father's arm. My father closed his eyes and said simply, "Locusts." The tone of his voice was one I had not heard before: one of helplessness and despair.

There was nothing anybody could do to stop the locusts from settling everywhere. The huge swarm reached our district just as the sun began to set. Millions of insects completely blotted out the sky. They were all heading in one direction, with their wings swishing and clicking noisily as they flew and fluttered low overhead in their relentless progress across the land.

Aubrey and I saddled the horses, took large nets with us and galloped up and down through the crops. My mother, father, the farmhands, Aubrey and I, yelled and beat drums and tin cans, but it was a lost battle. The swarm had flown a long way since it had risen that morning and was now tired and hungry and ready to settle.

As the sun sank beneath the horizon, the locusts simply folded their wings, dropped onto the ground and started eating every green shoot they found. The whole of the mountain and the veld beyond the river was covered in a brown, seething blanket of locusts two to three inches deep, all fighting to get to the green shoots. To chase them off the land was a hopeless task; eventually my parents gave up and sat dejectedly in the lounge and watched the locusts devour every blade of grass, every green leaf on the trees, and the remains of the wilting mielie crop.

Aubrey and I were still racing round on horseback, while the farmhands were shovelling locusts off the road into hundred-pound mielie sacks and carrying them back home to roast them for their evening meals. Locusts have little spikes on their long, hard back legs, and there is an art in collecting them without pricking yourself. You have to grasp them with finger and thumb at the base of their wings just behind their heads, to prevent their legs from kicking out and their spikes from drawing blood.

Soon it was too dark to see them and we could do no more except keep the windows and doors closed to stop these creatures from crawling inside the house. After supper Aubrey and I went down to Meofi and Mankahpa's hut to see what they were doing with the insects they had collected. The family was sitting in a group and removing the locusts' heads, wings and legs which they threw away. They put the locusts' bodies into a big pot to roast slowly over an open fire. Now and then a sprinkling of salt was added and the insects were given an occasional stir with a stick.

When the roasting was done, we sat in a circle round the fire with a bowlful of mieliemeel on the ground in front of us. Everyone then helped himself or herself to a couple of handfuls of roast locusts. We watched the family as they scooped up some thick mieliemeel porridge, rolled it into walnut-sized balls, chose a nice, fat locust and popped that into their mouths as well. The locusts sounded so crisp, crackly and crunchy and the family was enjoying them so much that we began to wonder what roast locusts really tasted like. Motorcar must have noticed us because she picked up a locust in each hand and offered one each to Aubrey and me. We were very hesitant at first but Meofi and Mankahpa, judging by the smacking of their lips, were obviously enjoying them so much that we gingerly took the proffered insects. At first it was as much as I could do to hold one, let alone taste it. However, Aubrey, not wanting to appear squeamish in front of Mankahpa, bit off the top half and started to chew. I felt sick as I looked at him, but then a smile spread over his face and he said, "It's nice, it's got a nutty flavour," and put the rest of it into his mouth. "Try it, Nancy, you'll like it," and he took a second one that was offered to him.

I sat pondering what to do. The locust was still held between my finger and thumb. I wished I had the courage to just pop it into my mouth, but could not bring myself to do so. Eventually Aubrey persuaded me to try a "tiny little bit, at first."

With a tremendous effort I lifted it to my mouth and bit off about a millimetre of the tail. I found it had indeed got a nutty flavour and was really very pleasant to taste and so, bit by tiny bit, I finished the whole thing, while Aubrey, who by now had been given a bowlful of his own, was really tucking into them. Eventually I threw off all inhibitions and enjoyed the feast as much as everybody else. My mother was horrified when we told her we'd dined on locusts.

Very early the next day we got up to see what damage had been done. The swarm, still a bit stupefied by the cold night air, was lying on the ground. However, when the sun rose over the horizon, the locusts, as if reacting to a military command, rose in one thick, dense brown cloud that soared higher and higher. Their under-wings flashed pinky-orange against the rising sun as they blotted out all daylight beneath them. Within an hour they had blurred into just another brown cloud which drifted away into the pastel shades of the early morning sky.

Behind them on most of the farms in the region, they had left only devastation. Hardly a green leaf or branch could be seen for many miles around. The remainder of the crops which had already wilted from the drought of the previous three years, had been eaten down to the ground.

My father looked tired and strained. He said, "Oh, well, hopefully we won't get another swarm for two to three years. I wonder where their next port of call will be. They've obviously come from the direction of the Kalahari but where do they end up after the Eastern Transvaal? There's only the Indian Ocean after that, so hopefully they'll all drown themselves!"

* * * * *

The Northern Transvaal was at that time a malaria-infested region. Each year hundreds of people died – particularly those who lived in very remote areas too far away from doctors and medical supplies. The malaria-carrying mosquito thrived in the hot, muddy pools and on the banks of the rivers.

We protected ourselves at night by sleeping under mosquito nets, which were always kept tidily knotted up above the bed during daylight hours but tucked in firmly all round the bed before sunset. We often lay on our beds, listening to the mosquitoes' high-pitched "pinnng" as they flew about in droves on the outside of the nets, trying to crawl through to us and feast on our blood.

At school, it was a different matter altogether. There we had no protection and were exposed to the mosquitoes' vicious attacks every night when they bit us mercilessly as we lay sleeping. Several children contracted malaria every year.

One day I began to feel cold and shivery in class. I asked to be excused and stood on the burning hot concrete on the verandah where I clung to a metal pole. It was so hot that the paint was beginning to melt but I could not face the cool classroom and just stood clinging on to the pole in the blazing sun. After some time a girl was sent out to look for me. She ran in to tell the teacher I was shivering and my teeth were chattering and that I had said I felt cold.

When Mr Van der Merwe came out and saw me, within minutes I was taken to the school sanatorium. There I was put to bed with a temperature of a hundred and four degrees Fahrenheit, shivering violently. The nurse piled blankets on top of me and still I shivered. I had a terrible headache.

I remember no more of the following three days as I lay delirious and desperately ill. A rider was despatched to call my parents to school. My father stayed with me for a day then left my mother at school to nurse me and help the overworked nurse look after the other children who had contracted malaria and were now in the sanatorium.

Several days after the onset of the fever, and as soon as my mother decided it would be safe to move me, I was taken home where gradually I was nursed back to health. I was very tired and very weak because I could not eat anything, and I lay in bed. My mother and Old John tried hard to cook something that they thought might whet my appetite but nothing seemed to tempt me to eat. The tiniest taste on my tongue brought a terrible feeling of nausea.

My parents became very worried as I was becoming much too thin. One lunch-time my mother brought in a small soup bowl of home-made chicken soup. She put the tray on my knee and said, "I've made a very nice soup and I'd like you to try to take a little, just for me."

I sat up and, not feeling at all hungry, dipped the spoon into the soup and tasted it. It was delicious. I finished a plateful and even asked for more, to my parents' delight. They sat on the bed watching me finish the second bowl of soup.

Gradually I began to return to normal health, though for weeks after that, my skin remained a deep, dark yellow which eventually faded away. I had lost a lot of weight and was very weak so I had to stay off school for the rest of the term. But I have never forgotten the taste of that bowl of my mother's chicken soup and even today I love soup of any kind.

* * * * *

It was the marula season. Aubrey and I knew of a very large marula tree which was always full of big, juicy fruit, right on the boundary of our farm.

One day we set off with some bags for the marula fruit. When we got there, the tree was full of monkeys, all busily picking and sucking the fruit, so we decided to wait till they had eaten their fill as nothing would persuade them to come down to make way for us. Crusoe, eager to chase them down from the tree, was straining at his collar, but we were afraid that such a large troop would attack him.

We sat for some time, hoping they would soon leave, but they were all so busy eating and playing around amongst the branches that it was obvious they had no intention of leaving the tree, so we had to move on. When we found a marula tree nearby, Aubrey said, "I'll climb up and pick them and throw them down to you." I stood underneath the tree in the very thick grass, catching the fruit. When my bag was full, Aubrey climbed down and we sucked marulas noisily as we sat down on an old tree stump.

Crusoe had been lying down quietly in the cool grass. After a while he got up and started sniffing around under the stump we were sitting on. Aubrey said, "He's probably found the scent of a meerkat or a lizard or something."

A slight movement caught my eye. I then noticed the grass at the other side of the log had been disturbed and saw something in the grass moving quite fast. I whispered to Aubrey, "There's something in the grass, Aubrey, at the end of the log at the other side." Meanwhile Crusoe appeared to be getting more excited and began to bark and scratch the dead leaves under the stump.

Aubrey first stood up then he knelt down, one hand resting on the stump, and with his face close to the ground, he started looking along the underside of the dead log. All of a sudden a big, black mamba very close to Aubrey's head crawled out, its neck bent back, ready to strike. Aubrey was still poking the stick about in the dead leaves under the stump.

I screamed, "Mamba! Run, Aubrey, quick! It's right above your neck!" Before he could move, Crusoe leapt right over the log and clenched the mamba a few inches below its head. It writhed and wriggled, its body thrashed round Crusoe's head but Crusoe held firm. His jaws, however, had locked just too far down the mamba's neck and the snake was still able to turn its head and sink its fangs deep into Crusoe's neck. He yelped but did not let go.

In a matter of seconds he began to froth at the mouth and wheeled round and round until his jaw slackened and the mamba fell out of his mouth. Crusoe fell down beside the snake. He had lost control of his muscles and his body twitched and jerked severely. He looked up at us and whined.

For a moment we stood there stupefied, then I turned and ran home as fast as I could, shouting for my father. He shook me, trying to understand what had happened. Between sobs I told him that Crusoe had been bitten by a black mamba. He quickly saddled his horse, collected his FitzSimmons snake bite kit and with me sitting in front of him in the saddle we galloped to the marula tree.

When we got there, we found Aubrey kneeling down and sobbing beside Crusoe whose now still body lay alongside the mamba. We could do no more for Crusoe, so we climbed up onto the saddle beside my father and rode home. Later that

161

afternoon we returned with my father and buried Crusoe underneath the marula tree. We could not be consoled and cried for many days. We had lost our best friend, our dog, Crusoe. He had died a hero's death.

* * * * *

Andries was now becoming too old to manage to do much work on the farm. It was time for Mankahpa to assume the responsibilities of the head of the household and the family decided to move out of the area to find a more sustainable type of job for him and possibly also for Meofi. The whole family, about twelve of them in all, packed their few belongings, left their huts and set off on foot to a location many miles away from us. We were very sad to see them leave, but we understood that they, like everyone else, had to move on.

CHAPTER 12
FAREWELL

The 1930s, the time of the Great Depression, were hard years. Farmers in the Northern Transvaal were severely affected by both the depressed state of the economy and the worst drought in living memory.

Rivers and muddy pools dried up and the few remaining barbel that had managed to survive, wriggling and thrashing about in the fast-drying mud, now lay motionless and stiff, their bodies scattered about on the surface of the hard, cracked earth. Animals walked slowly and wearily about, seeking what shade they could under withering little bushes. The hens, hoping to find cooler earth, stretched their wings and scratched hollows in the ground.

Month after month the Transvaal baked and shimmered in the relentless heat. Leaves and grass shrivelled up and turned brown. The drought had already lasted almost three years. The veld was bare, hard and dry. There was no fodder for the cattle. Crops failed to grow after the locusts had devoured the last few blades of grass and leaves still left. Cattle, now thin and weak, swished hordes of buzzing flies away with their tails and stood listlessly round the trough mercifully filled with water drawn up by the windmill. Malaria was claiming the lives of many thousands of people although we were fortunate as we were able to sleep under our mosquito nets every night on the farm.

My father, who was an asthmatic, and at sixty-eight no longer a young man, became tense, weary and ill with worry as he watched his good herd of Friesland cattle slowly grow thinner and weaker. Eventually they no longer had the strength to trail up to the water trough, so just fell and died in their tracks on the burning veld. The stench of rotting carcasses smothered the air. Vultures, hyenas, jackals and other scavengers feasted so well that they left many dead animals untouched. These carcasses dried out quickly in the sun and were eaten by ants and worms. Swarms of blowflies and bluebottles buzzed incessantly over the spoils.

One evening, after a particularly dry and hot day, we heard a muffled roar and crackle from across the flats. The

163

horizon glowed a dusty orange and the air was heavy with smoke from a veld fire that raced up the tinder-dry mountain. The fire destroyed everything in its path as it swept along, fanned by a strong evening breeze. Our homes lay directly in its path, so my father got out of his sick bed to organize the building of a wide firebreak around our house and the huts of the farmhands.

Aubrey and I caught and saddled our horses and galloped over the river and across the veld, to round up as many volunteers as we could to help build the fire break with sacks of sand. Everyone worked hard and fast, beating out the flames that were dangerously close to all our homes. Aubrey and I were kept busy damping down the sacks with water from the trough. We could hear the bleating of buck, the barks of the baboons and the squeals of smaller animals and birds that were trying to flee from the intense heat and flames.

The fire raged, crackled and roared across the mountain all night, the tall flames lighting up the whole area and staining the sky. The next morning the fire eventually burnt itself out, helped by a heavy dew that dampened down the bushveld.

When dawn broke we looked up at our mountain. Only the skeletons of charred and blackened trees were left standing: everything else had been destroyed. The smell of burnt flesh of animals and reptiles that were either too old, too young, too slow, too confused or too ill to escape, filled the air.

Later that morning Aubrey and I carefully picked our way over the still smouldering ashes, about half a mile up the mountain. All was very quiet; there was no sign of anything living – nothing but charred, dead reptiles and small animals. It was a depressing scene.

The mountain had died overnight.

* * * * *

Our home, which had been full of the sound of laughter and the hub of all the activity on the farm, was quiet. My mother spent her time in the bedroom, nursing my father. The news that he was very ill spread rapidly through the communities of black people, who had always liked him and held him in great respect.

One morning a small group walked up our driveway. Old John went to meet them, then came to my mother and said, "Missi, they hear the baas is velly sick and they have blought a witchdoctor with some medicine to make him better." My mother hesitated for a while, but my father said, "No, Mabel, the poor old blighter's walked a very long way to help me, so we must invite him in."

The witchdoctor's forehead was adorned with bird feathers and the claws and teeth of animals; he had dried beetles and porcupine quills round his neck, and from his waist down to his knees hung several jackals' tails, all of which gave off a very pungent smell. He was accompanied by a younger man with a small skin bag round his neck and carrying a leopard skin, tied together by its legs, and bulging with things for medicinal use. The witchdoctor greeted my father with a long, murmuring chant. He sat down in the middle of the bedroom floor, untied the leopard skin bag, took out all his medicines and placed them, one by one, at carefully chosen places in front of him. My father looked very bemused as he watched dried lizards' heads, dried seed pods, dried monkey paws, skulls, snake heads and tongues, ostrich and turkey feathers and several small bones of various shapes being placed on the floor. The witchdoctor then placed some small white feathers between his fingers, took a handful of knucklebones which he called "dollos", threw them vigorously across the floor in front of him towards my father's bed, then blew the feathers in the same direction. He chanted softly as he touched each dollos with his forefinger.

Once this ritual had ended, he gathered up all these objects and returned them to his leopard-skin bag. He told Old John that he would like two hairs from my father's head. These he carefully wrapped up in the small bag round his assistant's neck. The witchdoctor smeared some ointment on his thumb, took a few paces towards my father and touched him on his forehead with his sticky thumb, chanting as he did so, then said, "Uldumela Kgosi" and walked to the door. My father said to my mother, "Give the poor old blighter a cup of tea and some money as a thank you – he's walked a very long way, but tell John to get a bucket of water and some strong carbolic soap and wash the floor."

165

Despite everything, however, my father's health was rapidly deteriorating. He breathed with difficulty and grew weak and thin. All the hard work he had put into the farm, all his money, all his hopes and dreams for the place, had died. My father had filled the house: now both he and the farm were fading and eventually, one morning as he tried to get out of bed, he collapsed.

Aubrey immediately jumped in the Chevrolet and raced to Louis Trichardt, thirty-five miles away, to summon the doctor who came immediately, examined my father then gave him an injection and some pills. He told my mother that her husband had had a major heart attack and that he could not live longer than a few days.

My father died soon after this. His funeral was arranged by the doctor and the Anglican vicar from Louis Trichardt. Two days later Herbert and Molly arrived by train from Johannesburg. Aubrey drove us to Louis Trichardt to buy some mourning clothes. There were a few nice dresses and hats for my mother to choose from and she looked very stylish in her outfit. I had to wear a long black dress and an old-fashioned, black hat. I hated them both as I was still only fifteen.

On the day of the funeral Mr and Mrs Chomse drove my mother, Molly and me to the church in Louis Trichardt. Aubrey, Herbert and Old John rode in an open truck with the driver who had only the previous day brought the coffin to Dalemain from Louis Trichardt.

The western horizon was becoming very dark, which meant there was a heavy storm brewing. My mother, Molly and I arrived at the little church just as the large drops of rain that signalled the onset of the storm, began to fall. Thunderclaps grew louder and lightning flashed more brilliantly with every passing minute. It was almost pitch black in the church, and everything seemed ominous and unreal.

Not far from Dalemain when the storm had been at its fiercest, the truck carrying my father's coffin stuck fast in the mud. Aubrey, Herbert, Old John and the driver had to get out in driving rain and dislodge the wheels. An hour and a half later, very wet, muddy and tired, they arrived at the church. The wind had torn off the tarpaulin covering the back of the truck and exposed the coffin which was wet, dirty and heavily splashed with mud.

Black and white people travelled from farms many miles away to cram into the little church. Many of them came up to my mother to shake their heads sadly and say to her, "Hau! O kgwile, Missis." (He's dead). After the service we followed the coffin down to the cemetery half a mile from the church. My mother had no money to pay for a gravestone and Herbert and Molly felt it was not necessary to erect one. Instead his grave, amongst the old Voortrekkers' graves and some more recent ones, was marked with a number. His remains lie near the large granite memorial commemorating Louis Trichardt and the Voortrekkers.

As soon as news of my father's death became known, people from miles around came to pay their respects and to offer their condolences to my mother, Aubrey and me, as well as any help we might need. In fact, there was little they could do for us. Most of their own farms had also been devastated by drought, locusts and veld fires; people were struggling to cope with their own families' needs and were in no position to help us.

The day after the funeral, Dalemain was locked up and the keys were given to Old John who would be staying to look after the place till we returned, though we did not know when that would be. We left the next morning very early with Herbert and Molly for Benoni, three hundred miles away where, it had been decided, we were to stay with Robin and his wife.

After a few days in Benoni, Aubrey returned to the Soutpansberg to stay with the Chomses, to help Mr Chomse on his farm. Robin at this time was working as a miner on the Johannesburg gold mines; he was not well paid and his wife felt they could no longer support my mother and me as well as themselves.

Mr and Mrs Cheales and her family had moved to Johannesburg two years previously, and when they heard the news of my father's death, we went to stay with them for a while. Although they had little spare money, they were very kind to my mother and me but I longed so much for Dalemain and envied Aubrey when he came back to visit us with tales of the Soutpansberg.

One day Molly came to visit us at the Cheales's home and said to my mother that I should try to get a job in Johannesburg as the Chealeses were not rich and could not support us much longer. With that she went to the city to find me a job. She came back the next day with the news that there was a position in a general store called Cash & Carry in Bree Street, Johannesburg. I was to start work the very next morning as a lift girl since it was the only job they could offer an inexperienced girl of fifteen.

I had been used to the quietness and tranquillity of the bushveld and was very frightened of the noise and bustle of Johannesburg as Molly drove me through the city. We stopped in front of a huge shop and got out of her little car. She took me inside and introduced me to the store manageress, who shook my hand and then said, "Good morning, Miss Mathews. You will be our lift girl. Follow me." I was wondering what a Lift Girl was as I'd never heard of, let alone seen, a lift. The manageress introduced me to Dulcie, the current lift girl, and told her that I was the girl who was going to replace her, and that she had to show me how to operate the lift. Molly left and Dulcie ordered me to, "Kom!"

I followed her; she walked to the back of the store where she opened a little concertina door into the tiniest room I'd ever seen. There was just enough space for four people to stand up. Dulcie shut the metal concertina gate with a crash, pressed a handle and we shot upwards. I felt faint with fright. We stopped on the next floor with a jerk. Dulcie again flung the metal concertina gate back and a man stepped in and said, "Ground floor, please."

Dulcie turned the handle the opposite way and this odd little room went hurtling down again, then after a few jumps it stopped with a jerk. Dulcie again flung the metal concertina gate back and a man stepped in and said, "First floor, please."

Dulcie stayed with me for half a day while trying to show me how to operate this terrifying contraption. At twelve o'clock, she told me it was my lunch time and that I should go next door to the staff room where I'd get a free buttered roll and a cup of tea.

I ventured warily over to the staffroom, but when I got there, it was full of noisy young white men and women in front of the tea counter. They were all jostling, shoving and pushing each other for their tea and buns and were making so much noise clattering their trays and talking and shouting that there was no way I could get anywhere near the counter.

I had been taught never to push ahead of anyone, so I just stayed watching the spectacle for a few minutes then went back to the lift. Dulcie told me I'd been very quick – had I had my tea and bun? I answered yes, I had. She then told me, "Well, I'm going for my lunch, and then I'm going upstairs to do my new job behind the counter. Bye! Good luck!"

I was left alone and terrified. I simply hated it when the lift was called up to the second floor. I was always afraid that the steel ropes would snap and that the lift would go crashing down to the basement with me in it. I was nervous on each trip to the first floor, and terrified when we reached the second floor. I was thoroughly miserable and as the day went on, my fear became worse. Nor did it subside in time – I was as nervous at the end of the week as I had been at the beginning.

One afternoon at the end of the month I brought the lift down to the ground floor and was very surprised to see the manageress standing with Molly and another girl waiting for me outside the lift. The Manageress said to me, "Miss Mathews, this is Magrietha, who is going to take over from you as lift girl. Here is your pay." She handed me an envelope and said with a smile, "Thank you and goodbye. I hope you will be happy." Happy was the wrong word. Even though I had begun my working life by being sacked after less than one month, I was delighted and relieved.

With that Molly said, "Come on, Nancy, I'm taking you back to the Chealeses. I've arranged for you and your mother to go back to Dalemain tomorrow night by train. I think you'll all be much happier together there." When we got into her car she said, "Open your envelope and see how much they have paid you." I tore open the envelope and inside I found a crisp ten shilling note and two half crowns. Not having worked before I had no idea whether or not I had been well rewarded.

Next day my mother bought some provisions for our return to Dalemain: bread, sugar, rice, salt and flour. That evening after we said goodbye to Mr and Mrs Cheales, Herbert and Molly took us to Johannesburg station to catch the northbound train. The journey back was a blur of bare veld punctuated by stops at Pretoria, Pietersburg, Potgietersrus, Naboomspruit, Bandelierkop, and Solomondale before the train eventually ground to a halt at Louis Trichardt. Mr and Mrs Chomse met us at Louis Trichardt station and drove us back to Dalemain.

It was a quiet, sad homecoming. Old John and Maria came to meet us as we got out of the car with the greeting, "Velly preased you coming back, Missi, Basie and Nonnie. Evely ting is leddy for you." We all went inside where Maria had a nice cup of tea waiting for us. Everything was exactly as we'd left it.

It felt strange and unreal to be back. A place that had always been so happy, alive and full of fun now seemed forlorn, quiet, empty and different. Our lives had been fractured; we all felt the loss of my father very deeply. For the first time in my life, I felt isolated, vulnerable and afraid. For the first time in my life, I felt threatened by the bush and all the dangers that lurked there. A week later I returned to Happy Rest School while Aubrey and my mother stayed on at Dalemain for another few months.

The government proclaimed the whole of the Northern Transvaal a drought-stricken area. None of the local farmers, however loathe they might have been to leave their homes, could survive in such terrible conditions. One by one they sold those remaining thin, weak cattle which had miraculously managed to remain on their feet, packed up their few goods and chattels onto their wagons, locked the doors behind them and moved away. Some of them stayed with relatives while others moved to more prosperous areas to work as farmhands.

* * * * *

It was becoming increasingly evident that we could not support ourselves any longer. One day my mother told Aubrey and me that we would have to leave Dalemain. She said she was making arrangements to go back to live near her family in England.

Although we were very upset, we were old enough to understand that we would not be able to live on the farm any longer. Most other farmers had by now left the district. This left us more isolated than ever.

Our goods and chattels were to be sold after we left Dalemain. A solicitor who was one of Molly's friends from the Oxford Group, the religious organization with which she was heavily involved, was left to administer the estate. We packed up a few small things which were to be shipped to England and others which were to be sold: some family silver, crockery, table and bed linen. The proceeds of the sale were to be forwarded to my mother in England, but once again fate struck a cruel blow. Unbeknown to Molly and to us, the solicitor embezzled all the money from our sale and was bankrupted, apparently unable to repay anything. Nor were all of my father's possessions shipped back to England: years later, we saw a silver-handled regimental cane and some silver spoons displayed in a neighbour's house.

We were now destitute. We did not even have enough money to pay for the voyage, nor were Herbert, Molly and Robin able to help pay for our passage to England. My mother wrote to her eldest brother, Sam, who as the firstborn son had been given the best education of her family, and was by now a scientist of some repute in England, to ask if he could pay for our fares. Sam, who was later to become one of the suspects in the Piltdown Man hoax, refused. My mother wrote again, explaining that she was destitute. Sam grudgingly lent her £300, on the understanding that once Aubrey and I started working, we were to repay the debt.

Meanwhile, letters had passed between my mother and her sisters in Stainton near Penrith in the Lake District, where we were going to live for a while. Mail took several weeks to travel between South Africa and England. Although this inevitably complicated matters, eventually arrangements were made for us to sail from Cape Town on Christmas Eve, 1937. Our berths were booked on the Balmoral Castle.

* * * * *

Our last few days at Dalemain were quiet and sad since we knew that we would never live there again. We spent our time saying goodbye to the few families still left in the district: the Bells, the Eastwoods and one or two others. We took a last walk round all the old familiar places on the farm where we had played, had so much fun and spent so many carefree hours.

We paid one last visit to Crusoe's grave and we each carved our names on the marula tree where we had buried him. We stood a few minutes thinking of all the happy years we had shared, then we turned away, leaving him to rest in peace.

After breakfast we made a flag from an iron bar we found lying about in the garden and a strong piece of sail cloth which we sewed tightly with a sacking needle and twine onto the iron bar. We filled our bottles with lemon juice, made some sandwiches and then started up the mountain with the flag, which we were going to erect on the summit. On the way up we saw all the familiar animals and lizards, including our old friends, the baboons, who showed no compassion to us on this, our very last mission up into their own private domain. They kept up the feud with us and persisted on playing their irritating game of rolling rocks down on us. When they realised we were ignoring them, they moved past us further down the mountain, on their way to their playground beside the Hout River.

We continued our climb up the mountain, through the ravine and up and over precipices to the top. By then we were sweating and very tired, so we sat down and drank our lemon juice which had become very warm inside the tin containers. We ate some of our sandwiches and kept the remainder.

For some time we sat without talking and gazed at the familiar scene spread out below us. The view had never failed to thrill us, no matter how many times we had seen it, but now it was different. We knew that this time would be the last, for tomorrow we would be leaving.

We looked along the distant, hazy blue horizon. What lay beyond? we had so often wondered. Tomorrow we would know, because tomorrow we would ourselves be beyond horizon, hundreds of miles away from our mountain, which would itself then become the horizon, beyond reach and beyond sight. This thought filled us with renewed sadness.

After a short rest we began gathering together rocks and stones which lay scattered about the summit. We hammered the flag we'd made into the hard, rocky surface and banked it up securely with rocks and stones, so that neither wind nor storm could dislodge it. We knew it would be safe from monkeys and baboons as there were neither berries nor water to tempt them to venture so high up.

We had been so busy all day that we did not realize how late it was until we noticed the long shadow of the mountain stretching out towards the east. Fish eagles were calling forlornly to one another as they returned from their daily fishing along the river, which was now much further away because the severity of the drought had forced them to change course. We climbed down the precipice, through the ravine and thick bush and down the long, steep slope to the house.

At the back door we turned and looked up at the flag. It was gaily fluttering in the evening breeze, white against the darkening sky.

While we were up on the mountain, Old John had been preparing our supper and also the food we would need for the first night of our journey. My mother had finished packing and lined the cases up in the lounge. The house looked very bare, and our voices echoed hollow in the empty rooms. I remember thinking they sounded like lost souls seeking refuge.

We slept fitfully that night and woke up very early. I looked down towards the hen run and the roosting tree. It was deserted: everywhere round the house was very quiet and deserted, too. The only sound was that of the guinea-fowl who called incessantly to each other across the river, far away.

While we were having our breakfast, Old John came into the dining-room and said, "Somebody to see you at the back door, Missis." We all got up to see who it was. There stood a solemn little group of our farm workers, men, women and children, young and old. My mother asked, "What do they want, John?" He said, "They don' want you to go away, Missis, they want you to stay and me too, I don' want you to go away."

173

My mother said, "John, I can't stay. I've got no money now and I won't be able to pay any of you for work you do for me."

He translated this to the little group behind him, and after some discussion, said, "They say they don' want money, they and me too wi' work for you for no money, but preez don' go."

My mother was so deeply touched by this that she had to turn away. She came back a little later with some bundles of clothing that we would not need in England, and handed each person something. Everyone was very pleased, but did not mask their sadness at our departure. They all sat quietly on the stone wall in a dejected little group, till we left.

That morning the mountain was shrouded in thick mist. Aubrey and I waited and watched, hoping it would clear before we left. Eventually the cloud base lifted to reveal the sun riding high in the sky.

We sat down and waited for Mr and Mrs Chomse, who were taking us to Louis Trichardt to catch the early afternoon train to Johannesburg – the first stage of the long journey ahead of us. After what seemed an eternity, we heard their car chugging noisily up the driveway.

Just before we left Dalemain, we looked up at the mountain and saw the last little wisp of lacy mist rolling away over the top, leaving the whole mountain clear and bright. Aubrey and I cupped our hands and shouted, "Goodbyeee!" Back came the reply: "Goodbyeee!" Then we shouted, "We'll come back!" and the echo reverberated, "Come back! Come back!"

My mother called us, as we were already later setting off later than we had intended. We all climbed into the car. The solemn little group of farm workers climbed off the stone wall where they had been waiting patiently and stood beside the car where they called, "Goodoo bye my Missis, Baasie and Nonnie!"

Old John held on to the car door handle. Tears were streaming down his face. The little group of people waved and shouted and ran behind the car until it began to gather speed and left them all behind, to be quickly lost to view in the thick cloud of dust which swirled up behind the car.

With tear-stained faces we looked back and gave them a final wave, but by the time the dust had settled again, they were so far behind that we could make out only some indistinguishable shapes turning back round the bend and out of sight.

On our way to Louis Trichardt we passed deserted farmhouses which had belonged to farmers who had already packed up and left. We drove past groups of little children; some were busy making clay oxen and others were picking berries. The children stood up and waved as we passed, then settled down again to their toy-making and berry picking. The painfully thin cattle and goats they were herding picked at the stubbles of grass nearby.

Eventually we reached Louis Trichardt. We drove down the main street, past the Dutch Reformed church with its tall spire adorned with a weathercock, then down the hill to the railway station.

The train was already waiting, steam hissing out of one funnel and smoke belching from another. We lifted our cases out of the car and packed them all away under the seats of our compartment.

We just had time to say our goodbyes to Mr and Mrs Chomse when a whistle blew and we felt the train jerk. We were leaving. We waved till the train turned the bend, then we settled down for the journey, Aubrey and I in the window seats. After leaving the station, the train straightened out and we began our long journey across the shimmering Springbok Flats. An hour or so later my mother said, "Oh, look, we're beside Bristows Koppies." We peered out of the window and, sure enough, we were actually passing behind the koppies on the horizon we had so often looked at from Spitskop. Now that we were close beside them they looked so big and different, not the mere humps we had believed them to be when we had gazed at them from a distance.

Aubrey said, "We must be on the horizon now. Let's look across and see if we can see Dalemain and Spitskop." We all looked across and saw our mountain clearly silhouetted against the late afternoon sky. It looked small and so far away.

As the train puffed and chuffed noisily along, we kept looking back towards Spitskop. Slowly it began to recede and fade as the sun dipped behind the Blouberg mountains. We watched the colours change from golden brown to azure, then

175

melt into the deep, dark blue of the distance as night closed its black curtain across the sky.

We stared out of the window as the stars began to appear. We recognised the Southern Cross, Orion's Belt, The Plough and the Seven Sisters which my father had so often pointed out to us in the evenings when we sat on our verandah gazing over the veld.

As we were beginning to feel hungry, my mother brought out the food and Thermos flasks that Old John had prepared for us. We all enjoyed the chicken and ham sandwiches and the cups of tea. Shortly afterwards the bedding steward came round with large bundles of sheets, pillows and blankets and made our beds. At last we all climbed into our bunks, tired and weary after such a long, busy and exhausting day. We slept soundly that night.

Early the next day we arrived at Johannesburg station. Herbert met us and took us to Robin's house where we would stay until we caught the train at six o'clock the next evening on a three-day journey to Cape Town.

The scenery on the journey through the dry, flat Karoo looked the same for hundreds of miles. As far as we could see all around, small dry brown scrub bush, or Karoo bossies, grew out of the crusty, red and windswept ground. There were neither trees nor shade of any kind to give shelter from the burning rays of the sun. Here and there a small koppie punctuated the monotonous scene.

Occasionally we saw a few springbok pronking and flocks of ostriches with their wings stretched out to cool themselves, pecking about in the scrub. Tortoises at the side of the railway track tried in vain to climb over the sleepers. Once we left the Karoo behind us, the scene changed completely. High, blue mountains swept down into vast, lush green valleys bursting with vineyards and orange groves. Sparkling waterfalls cascaded down the mountainsides, and fell in a frothy spray into rocky pools hundreds of feet below. The railway line snaked through the mountains, twisting and turning, curving and doubling back on its downward journey. Sometimes, as the train manoeuvred the sharp bends, we could see the engine and several of the front carriages opposite us across a deep gorge, the gaping chasm that separated the front and rear carriages.

We eventually rounded the last curve and there spread out below us was the city of Cape Town, bathed in the warm, mellow afternoon sun. The cream-painted houses with red roofs dotted amongst tall, green trees festooned with brilliant flowers were a picture postcard. Beyond the city we saw, for the first time, the sea shimmering away to the horizon. We were thrilled at the sight - we had never imagined there could be so much water.

The train slowed down as we entered the docks, then after stopping and starting, puffing, hissing and shunting, it finally came to a standstill close to a vacant berth. A porter came towards us and took our luggage. He asked, "Where to, Medem?"

My mother replied, "The Balmoral Castle, please."

He looked at us for a while, then said, "But Medem, the Balmoral has already left one and a half hours ago."

My mother was shocked and bewildered. She said to the porter, "Is there a Union Castle office nearby?"

He said, "Yes, Medem, I will take you," and with that, he trundled our luggage off on a trolley. We followed him disconsolately. When we got to the office, my mother explained to the clerk what had happened and asked what he suggested we should do. He was very helpful: he phoned the purser of the Edinburgh Castle, explained our predicament and asked if he had any berths vacant on his ship. The purser apologetically told him the Edinburgh Castle was full.

After several phone calls, he came back to us and said, "The only thing we can offer you is one double and one single berth on the Dunbar Castle, which is sailing at six am tomorrow – she's due to dock in number four berth this afternoon. If you would like, I can get you onto her this evening, but she has temporarily been commandeered as a troop ship to carry almost a full complement of soldiers from Mauritius back to England. However, they can let you have a private section for you and your children."

There was nothing else we could do, so my mother said she would gladly accept it and thanked him for all the trouble he had taken for us. He suggested that we have a bus trip into Cape

Town and handed my mother some money for our lunch "with compliments from the Union Castle line."

We caught a bus to Adelaide Street, had some lunch and looked at the tempting displays in the shop windows. Everything looked so colourful; shrubs and tall, lilac jacaranda trees lining the streets were out in full bloom, the cream buildings were all fresh and clean, while Table Mountain towered majestically behind this lovely city.

After a few hours we returned to the docks, collected our luggage and waited at the terminal while the Dunbar Castle slowly edged her way into her berth.

At last, weary and tired in the late afternoon, we walked behind the porter who was carrying our luggage up the gangplank. We were taken down into our cabins. The little rooms looked so small and strange. I looked out of the porthole – instead of the brown, dry veld and bush we had known all our lives, we now looked onto miles and miles of sea stretching away to the horizon. I felt overwhelmingly sad.

We ate well, then feeling very tired, went to bed. We woke up early next morning to the sound of a bugle playing the Reveille, a reminder that we were on a troop ship. It was Christmas day and the beginning of a long, three-week sea voyage.

The following day brought a frenzy of activity on the ship as well as on shore. After a hearty but noisy breakfast surrounded by soldiers, we went up on deck and looked down onto the quayside. Everyone was bustling around, loading boxes and crates of military supplies onto the Dunbar Castle. Eventually, all the frantic activity on the quayside below the ship ceased, the gangways were hauled up, hatches were closed and the ropes tying the ship to bollards were slipped off. People started throwing streamers from ship to shore and back.

Gently the Dunbar Castle edged away. I felt very sad when I realised we were no longer on South African soil. The ship turned slowly and then headed out into the Atlantic. A band struck up and played, "Will Ye No Come Back Again". I made a secret vow that one day I would return. We stood on deck looking back, watching Table Mountain grow hazier and smaller till it appeared to sink into the sea.

The ship was full of soldiers, boisterous, noisy and rough. We were kept apart from them as we had our own little sun deck, while the soldiers enjoyed the largest part of the recreation decks. We often sat and watched them practising their drills three times every day. However, we didn't speak to them, nor they to us. Nonetheless, somehow or other Aubrey and one of the younger soldiers got into a fight which had to be stopped by the Commanding Officer. The young soldier was reprimanded and ordered not to go near the private passengers' quarters again.

The voyage continued smoothly till we entered the dreaded Bay of Biscay. I looked out and saw at one moment, mountainous seas towering far above our ship, while the next moment we were swept out of the trough and high up above the waves. I was terrified. The ship was being thrashed about like a cork in a whirlpool. We could not have any of our meals in the dining-room as plates, cups and cutlery raced from end to end of the table and eventually crashed onto the floor. We were served with sandwiches and bottles of liquid until the seas calmed down.

The three weeks' crossing was on the whole pleasantly uneventful, with deck games and occasional dances and parties. We arrived at Southampton, England, on 17th January, 1938. My mother was fifty-five years old, Aubrey seventeen and I was sixteen. We had travelled from a brilliant African midsummer to an English midwinter, bitterly cold with a grey sky and a blizzard swirling about the quayside. I was miserable and wanted to go back home. Silently I prayed that I would not have to live in such bleak surroundings for too long.

* * * * *

The blizzard had subsided but it was still icy cold when we docked at Southampton. We walked down the gangway and told a porter waiting to take our luggage that we wanted to get the next train to London. He took us to the platform and said that the train would not be long as it was the next one due in. My mother tipped him and he left.

Shortly afterwards, the train arrived and hurtled towards London. We got off at Waterloo station and went to an enquiry counter to ask where we would find somewhere to stay for the night. The young receptionist gave us the address of a bed-and-breakfast run by her aunt not far away. As it was midwinter and all the Christmas and New Year festivities were over, we had no problem in finding lodgings. The landlady said she had two rooms available and took us up three flights of stairs. We found the rooms to be reasonable so we put our cases down, locked the doors, then went out to buy ourselves some winter coats, jerseys, gloves and scarves. We were nearly frozen as we had only the very light clothing we had been wearing in the South African midsummer that we had just left behind. We were very glad to get back to the warmth of the boarding house and after a good evening meal and a bath and exhausted, we climbed straight into bed.

Next morning we caught a bus to Euston station and booked our seats on the two o'clock train to Penrith. We looked round a few shops nearby, had a cup of tea and sandwiches in a little corner café, then made our way to the platform. We settled down on the two o'clock train which groaned and squealed out of Euston. Once out of London, it picked up speed and went so fast that I was very scared and felt certain we were on a runaway train. Buildings, lampposts and signposts flew past and the compartment rocked from side to side.

These were so different from South African trains, which had engines twice the size of the little English engines yet were very much slower, and which pulled many more coaches. We had some coffee and sandwiches that the waiter brought round to the compartments. It began to grow dark at four o'clock and we could see little at all outside except for the small stations that the train flew through. Eventually the guard announced, "Penrith! Penrith!" We collected our luggage and waited till the train came to a halt. Neither Aubrey nor I could stop our teeth from chattering loudly in the taxi to Aunt Pat's old home in Stainton.

Stainton was a small, pretty little old farming village close to Ullswater. My mother's two other sisters, Clara and Mary, and her brother, Fred, lived in The Poplars at the top end of the village. The following day, as we walked up through the village to meet Aunts Mary and Clara and Uncle Fred, we noticed the corners of curtains of several houses being lifted a little and

180

saw faces staring out at us. We seemed to have aroused much local curiosity. When we looked back at the windows, the faces quickly disappeared and the corners of the curtains straightened until we passed by them, when they would again flick open.

Since we had been used to friendly greetings being extended to all strangers in South Africa, we considered the villagers' behaviour to be very odd indeed. Aubrey and I even found it funny to see faces popping in and out behind net curtains. When we told my mother this, she answered, "Well, you know, these village people all live a very quiet and confined life and aren't used to seeing people from other countries in their midst so they're naturally curious to see what South Africans look like. Don't worry – eventually they'll get used to us." I began to understand why my father had felt the need to escape from the confines of rural England.

My teeth were still chattering and I was shivering visibly, and so were Aubrey and my mother. We reached the door of The Poplars and knocked on the door. Aunt Mary opened it and said, "Well, you might have told us when you were coming," and with that, she took us in to the sitting-room where a fire was burning in the grate. I was so cold that I would have loved to sit down on top of the fire. We were given a steaming meal before we had to face the rigours of washing in a freezing bathroom.

Next morning I woke early and looked out of the window. Everything was blanketed in a thick covering of snow. I'd heard about snow but had never seen it and had not been able to imagine what it was like. Shivering and shaking, my hands blue with cold, I stood and gazed out at this strange spectacle. What a contrast it was to the hot and brilliantly colourful mornings we had always known. I felt terribly homesick.

We stayed at The Poplars for a month. My mother and I went to Carlisle in order to find work nursing at Warwick Square Nursing Home, the private nursing home where she had nursed during the First World War and where she had met my father.

She asked the matron, Miss Cardwell, who also owned the nursing home, if I could be employed there as a nurse. My mother explained that we had just come from South Africa and she hoped I might develop an interest in nursing and eventually do my training. Miss Cardwell was very understanding and I was engaged to start work the following Monday. I nursed there for nearly three years. It was in this nursing home, years later, that I met the man I married, Bewsher Smith, in the same room where twenty or so years previously my mother had met my father.

Nancy, Mabel, Aubrey. England.

That September we heard the news that Britain had declared war on Germany. It was a chilling thought.

I enjoyed nursing at Warwick Square. Miss Cardwell told my mother that she felt I ought to train to become a registered nurse. Unfortunately as I had left school at the age of fifteen, I did not have the necessary entrance qualifications. However Miss Cardwell spoke to a surgeon she knew, who was able to put in a personal recommendation for me to begin training as a nurse at Preston Royal Infirmary. I was accepted and in 1941 I left Warwick Square Nursing Home.

Shortly after, my mother was employed by a wealthy family in Cumberland as their private nurse. She travelled with the family occasionally to places as far away as Peebles in Scotland. Aubrey meanwhile enlisted as a rear gunner in the Royal Air Force.

CHAPTER 13
THE RETURN

For the next twenty years we lived in England. The Second World War began and ended, I completed my three and a half years' nursing training and Aubrey joined the Royal Air Force. After the war first Aubrey, then I, married and had children. Aubrey lived in Cornwall, while I remained in Cumberland where my two daughters, Vivien and Hilary, were born.

I tried very hard to settle down to the English way of life, but I still longed

Bewsher and Nancy Smith

for the African bushveld where life had been so different, so carefree and happy. Try as I might, I could not look on England as my home and I often felt very homesick.

My mother lived happily with my husband, Bewsher, and me in our house in Wigton. She was a wonderful grandmother and spent nearly every evening reading stories to Vivien who used to sit very still on her knee or lie down beside her on the bed and become totally absorbed in the story. When Hilary was born, my mother looked after both little girls, read to them and, despite having severe arthritis, often played with them. She also helped to nurse Hilary who, like my father, suffered from asthma. In 1954 my mother became very ill with infective colitis which she had contracted while living at Dalemain, and which had remained dormant for many years. Four weeks later she died in Carlisle Infirmary. She had been our mainstay and was very much missed by all of us.

183

Ten years after Bewsher and I married, his business ran into difficulties and we decided to make a fresh start, which meant emigrating to South Africa. While he was selling the house and all the excess furniture, Vivien, Hilary and I went to stay in Cornwall, near Aubrey and his family. Bewsher had lived all his life in Wigton and was very well known, so we expected the sale of our four-bedroom, detached house to be well attended and to attract several offers. The saleroom was packed, yet not one bid was made for the house – everyone had come out of curiosity. The house was put on the market once again and this time it did sell, though at a loss. In March 1957 Bewsher joined us in Cornwall before we caught the train to Southampton. Under the "1820 Settlers" scheme to assist immigrants to South Africa, we had been granted a passage on the Winchester Castle, an ocean liner of 20,001 tons.

Bewsher's sisters, Winifred and Dorothy, travelled to Southampton docks to bid us a tearful farewell. Bells, hooters and whistles were all clamouring together while the ship's band played "A Life On The Ocean Wave". Passengers and their friends and relations on shore threw streamers to each other. The colourful strips of paper were caught and held until the widening gulf finally snapped the paper. We stood on the deck and waved to Winifred and Dorothy as the ship very gently left her berth, and we watched the gap between ship and shore grow ever wider. It reminded me of my last voyage in 1937, when we had been bound for Southampton on board the troop ship, the Dunbar Castle.

I was very sad at leaving Aubrey in England, but he hoped that it would not be long before he and his family would also emigrate to a better life in South Africa.

It was a cold, grey day. A strong wind blew rain across the decks and blurred the outlines waving on the quayside. The Winchester Castle gathered speed and began to move out of the harbour to the open sea. Soon the small figures standing on the quayside were swallowed up in the gathering fog and gloom, so we went into the lounge to shelter from the bitter wind and driving rain.

The crossing was one of the foggiest on record. The foghorn sounded constantly from the Bay of Biscay all the way to Cape Town, but apart from this we enjoyed a smooth and happy voyage. We were one of a number of families who were emigrating to South Africa or Southern Rhodesia, and the atmosphere on board was happy and optimistic. Nearly everyone joined in the organized games and entertainment: the Crossing of the Line ceremony at the equator, the fancy dress parade and the Captain's dinner dance. I enlisted the help of some friends and together we made a Christmas tree costume for Vivien. Unfortunately we had forgotten to cut out holes for her eyes, so a stewardess had to lead a sightless Christmas tree round the lounge. We won first prize for the Most Original Fancy Dress.

Two weeks after leaving Southampton we arrived at Cape Town. The Winchester Castle was due to dock at six o'clock in the morning but she had to drop anchor three miles outside the harbour because the fog was still very dense. Even while the ship was out at anchor, her foghorn sounded warnings, which echoed mournfully across the bay every minute.

Suddenly at three in the afternoon the fog lifted and revealed majestic Table Mountain, looking exactly as it had when we left Cape Town twenty years before. I knew I was back home again. Robin and his wife were on the quayside to meet us and spent their annual holiday sailing with us on the Winchester Castle up to Durban.

We stayed in Cape Town for three days and explored the sights of that wonderful city. On the third day we set sail from Cape Town. A day or so later we docked in Port Elizabeth and East London before we disembarked in Durban harbour after a long but very happy, memorable and enjoyable three weeks at sea. Vivien and Hilary were in tears; they had had such a happy time and made so many friends that they did not want to leave the ship. We were met at the quayside by Herbert and his wife and family. His wife took the children to the beach while Herbert helped Bewsher and me sort out some documentation in Durban. We then drove on to our new home, which was a rented cottage on Herbert's farm, twenty-four miles from Durban. Bewsher worked for a while in Herbert's security business. This was not easy as Bewsher often had to walk four miles across African dust roads from the nearest village to the farm, after he had caught the bus back from Durban. After a few weeks Herbert's wife told us that it was time that we found accommodation of our own. It had

185

in any case become apparent that our future lay in Durban so we moved into two bedrooms in the Avenida, a small residential hotel in Florida Road, Durban.

Our first priority was for Bewsher and me to find new jobs. Bewsher soon secured a position as Company Secretary in a boat-building firm, Fred Nicholls (Pty) Ltd, where he worked for twenty years. Vivien and Hilary settled happily into Morningside Government School in Durban. Our first eighteen months in Durban were spent in the Avenida Hotel in the company of Rhodesian students, immigrant families and an assortment of white single people. However, the children needed the freedom of a home so we decided to rent a flat, 6 Lyme Hall, two blocks away from the Avenida Hotel.

This was a difficult time for us all. Initially I worked as a nurse in charge of Innes Road Nursing Home, which cared for the elderly mentally ill. It was a depressing experience. I was shocked: the patients were often ill-treated and humiliated by the untrained staff, and were expected to survive on very little food; the place was dirty and stank of urine. I soon came to the conclusion that I had no option but to retrain, as my British nursing qualifications were not accepted by the South African authorities. After a couple of years, I passed my final South African nursing examinations at Addington Hospital.

In time we grew to love Durban where we were to live for the next thirty years. It was a green and colourful, warm, clean and attractive city. One year after our arrival in South Africa, I received a letter from Aubrey which said that he and his family had decided to emigrate and would be joining us in Durban in three months' time. I could hardly wait for the time to pass. A few weeks later, Aubrey and his family arrived on Durban docks on the coldest, wettest and windiest day we had known in Durban. I quickly assured them all that this weather was very alien to Durban's hot, humid climate.

Aubrey worked on Herbert's farm as farm manager, before he was appointed Compound Manager at Herbert's security firm. Eventually he and his family also moved to Durban.

Aubrey and I often used to talk about going back to visit our old farm, Dalemain, in order to recall our happy childhood and teenage years. We had not forgotten our tryst with

Spitskop Mountain and how the answering echo of "Come back, come back" sounded so clearly the morning we left Dalemain. A couple of years after Aubrey's return to South Africa, we started to make plans to visit Mara and Spitskop during the children's summer holidays of 1959.

Very early one morning just as dawn was breaking, we set off in two cars on a journey of several hundreds of miles north. We wanted to be well on our way before the sun rose and became too hot for comfortable travelling. As we drove northwards, we heard the dawn chorus of the birds, monkeys and other small bush creatures that were squeaking, singing and chattering together.

We travelled fast along the grey glass-smooth road through Natal, past the green hills and hollows of the Valley of a Thousand Hills. We sped through several small hamlets and larger towns still waking to the African sunrise. We passed through the town of Ladysmith which nestles in the foothills of the mighty Drakensberg range, then up the long, steep climb to Van Reenen's Pass at the top of the mountain. Here we stopped to let the engines cool down and to admire the magnificent view of the ravine that plunged thousands of feet below the road. At the bottom of the ravine we could see, glinting in the sunlight, the rusty, burned-out relics of a few cars which had smashed onto the rocks at the bottom. It was an awesome and sobering sight.

Soon after leaving Van Reenen's Pass, we crossed the Natal border into the Orange Free State and continued along the highway till we reached Harrismith, a hot, dusty little town which lay sweltering in the sun, about two hundred and fifty miles north of Durban. We filled up with petrol, water and oil and found a pleasant little restaurant where we had breakfast. We sat outside for a little while and discussed the journey ahead as we made plans for our next stop in Pretoria that night. At midday we pulled up beneath a shady tree along the roadside and had a picnic. The children played at the roadside while the adults rested in the noonday heat.

Much refreshed, we climbed into our cars for the second stage of our journey. By nine in the morning the sun was already high and the arrow-straight Free State road lay before us.

187

Melting tarmac glistened towards the horizon and for hundreds of miles beyond.

After Ladysmith and as far as Harrismith, the land on both sides of the road lay flat and uninhabited. Shortly after leaving Harrismith, the view changed: here and there, small mountains that changed colour as the sun shone on them, jutted out of the veld. Later in the day, the landscape flattened and dust devils gathered up sand, leaves and grass and chased each other over the dry, furrowed earth beside the tarmac. We were caught in the middle of one of the these dust devils as it crossed the road and swirled and danced away in a frenzy across the parched, barren veld.

The sensible driver will cross the Orange Free State road as fast as he can since it is so easy to be hypnotised by the heat and seduced by monotony and exhaustion into falling asleep at the wheel. We made sure that both drivers were kept alert by being given a constant supply of fruit, cold drinks, sweets and biltong.

After two and a half hours of travelling at high speed we left the Free State behind us and reached the great Vaal River which marks the border of the Transvaal. Here the scenery became greener and more interesting.

The freeway bypassed several small towns. We saw Heidelberg away to our right. We would have liked to pull up there for a drink, but as by then it was already late afternoon, we decided instead to head straight for Pretoria and stop there for the night. From Heidelberg onwards the road became much busier, as this was the main highway leading to Johannesburg and Pretoria. We skirted the Golden City on our left, as we did not want to become enmeshed in rush hour traffic jams.

The scenery changed: the landscape was littered with mine dumps, mining buildings and factories. Even here, on the twenty-mile stretch between the two cities, the traffic was very heavy. We were all by now very weary and looking forward to arriving in Pretoria, a serene and tranquil city, before dark. Its wide streets were lined on either side with purple and pink jacaranda and scarlet flamboyant trees, all very tall and in full bloom.

We drove round, trying to find some inexpensive lodgings. The white people on the streets of Pretoria were dressed much more conservatively than those in Durban and our girls in shorts and sandals attracted several shocked stares from prim, sun-tanned Afrikaans ladies in crimplene dresses, white high heels and nylon stockings. Eventually we found a hotel, had a bath and a meal and slept soundly all night.

We left next morning at sunrise. Ahead of us stretched yet another hot journey of about three hundred miles to Louis Trichardt at the foot of the Soutpansberg.

I was unable to recognize much of the road from Pretoria to Pietersburg as we had very seldom travelled along that road before. We passed several beehive-shaped huts, and occasionally also villages and small towns. Pietersburg had changed greatly. When I had visited it as a child, it had been a small, slow and sleepy little town with a few shops and a small hotel. Ox and donkey wagons laden with grain, salt or corundum used to creak through the streets. By 1960 it had become a busy metropolis supporting its own university. Bicycles and cars clogged the roads and tinny juke boxes played in the cafes and tea-rooms on the main road. Carefully we threaded our way through the traffic.

From the town centre we turned off onto the Great North Road which was now tarred, though much the same as we remembered it, and I looked forward to the journey to Louis Trichardt. We passed several little roadside stalls bulging with oranges, naartjies, prickly pears, paw-paws and mangoes.

Ahead of us on our left, loomed the tall, rounded koppie where as children travelling with my mother and father in the donkey wagon, we used to pull up on our way to Pietersburg and outspan for the night.

We stopped the cars. Aubrey and I got out and climbed up the koppie. Very little vegetation grew on this huge single mound of rock, where a few leguaans had always lain warming themselves on the flat top. Aubrey and I used to enjoy disturbing them by poking them awake with a stick. They would react by turning clumsily round, open their mouths and hiss loudly, but as they were so slow on their stubby little legs, we were half way down the rock before they had turned round completely.

189

This time there were no leguaans to disturb, and the children ran freely up and down the rock face.

After passing the rock, we continued towards Louis Trichardt. The road was very straight, and stretched away towards the Soutpansberg mountain range till it looked like a piece of cotton threaded over the horizon. The area on either side of the road was very flat and dry. As far as we could see, yellow stubble grass grew in between small, brown thorn-bushes, on which a few thin cattle, donkeys and goats nibbled.

As we journeyed towards the horizon, we could see for the first time the hazy, blue outline of the Soutpansberg range. We knew then that we were nearing home but even though Aubrey and I strained to see, we could not as yet make out Spitskop which was still hidden in the shadow of the Soutpansberg.

We drove on for another hour. Slowly the jagged peak of Spitskop became faintly visible, then suddenly emerged as though stepping forwards out of time to greet us. What a thrill it was to see the outline of our mountain again! As the sun was beginning to set and as we were all very hungry, we decided to find rooms for the night. Even though we had travelled so far, Spitskop was still thirty-five miles away.

We booked into the hotel where we had stayed when we accompanied my father to buy or sell stock. Hotel Louis had retained its high, cool, white ceilings and the large verandah with shiny, red-cement floors. The dining-room was still furnished with deeply polished oak tables covered with starched white table-cloths and heavy silver cutlery. We were in a time-warp: the colours, the smells – nothing had changed.

The following morning we continued on the last part of our journey to Spitskop. The road from Louis Trichardt had not changed much in our twenty-year absence, except for one area where some bush had been cut away to straighten a bend. One or two red-roofed houses were still tucked into the foothills of the mountain. Hot little Mara station had grown a little, as there were a few more asbestos huts scattered about. Further along the road a few huts had vanished, but others had been built.

Sand River was still only a stream flowing in a wide, sandy bed, spanned by the old, iron bridge. It no doubt still had to cope with flash floods caused by the summer rains when everything in the path of the torrent of water was savagely swept away.

After we had crossed the bridge we turned off the main road and through the thick bush, onto a stony, dusty little track which followed Hout River, now just a dry, bushy ravine with a small, muddy pool fed by a trickle of water. Tick birds and guinea-fowl were standing in and around the pool and pecking each other for a better position as they lowered their heads and scooped up water with their beaks.

The sun was white-hot as we drove on towards Spitskop. We passed the thickets where we used to gather wild berries, and the rocks where we used to chase the meerkats into their holes then hide and wait for their heads to pop up again.

We stopped the cars and walked across to Dado's grave. The stones we had put on top of the grave were still there, but had now sunk below ground level, partially hidden by some thorn-bushes.

A little further on we started to look for the twisting path which my father had built from the road up to the house. Suddenly Aubrey spotted a long, narrow ravine with rocks and stones covered by thick thorn-bush. We followed this a little way as we felt sure that it was the road my father had built, but we guessed that with the passing of years it must have been washed away by heavy streams of rain water gushing down from the mountain.

We retraced our steps and drove back further along the road. The bush had grown so thick and tall that we had to search hard to locate any landmarks. Eventually, we discovered at the roadside, our old post-box, knocked to the ground and now forming a rotting, ant-eaten heap which was mostly covered by bush. Beside it, a narrow track had been channelled through thick undergrowth and over boulders and dead tree stumps. We climbed out of the cars. The slamming of the car doors jarred against the impenetrable stillness of the bush. Aubrey led the way through the undergrowth and viciously curved thorn-bushes that barricaded the path, over large boulders and dead tree stumps. The path widened, turned a final bend and suddenly we were confronted by a mass of red, round stones scattered in heaps over

191

the ground: the remains of the wall that my father had built round the house.

Aubrey pointed to a tall acacia tree surrounded by a little heap of stones and said, "Look! This must be the acacia seed we planted in our rockery at the corner of the house – remember?"

"Yes, I remember planting it," I said

We peered past the acacia tree to the right, where we recognized the foundations of the house where grass now grew in between large jagged slabs of concrete. Forlorn little piles of bricks lay strewn in front of the foundations – a sad reminder of a once happy home. Strangely enough the steps leading down to the cellar under the foundations were all still intact and littered with some skulls and animal bones.

Sitting on top of the foundations of Dalemain was a small hut with walls of baked mud and a corrugated iron roof, propped up by large wooden poles. Two shy little white children, barefoot and in ragged clothes, stared at us then ran through the lean-to door into the hut. Several other children ran out from the back of the hut, and scattered dogs and cats and the hens that were peacefully pecking in the red dust. A pig snuffling at the front of the house squealed and trotted into the bush. The door swung back uneasily on its one remaining hinge and a fat, dirty and heavily pregnant white woman of about my age appeared.

She greeted us politely and looked at us enquiringly. "Goeie môre."

Aubrey returned the greeting and explained that we were revisiting the area. The woman looked at Aubrey and then at me intently for a few seconds, then said, "O ja, ek ken haar. Dis Nancy Mathews." (Oh yes, I know her – it's Nancy Mathews.)

I looked blankly at the stranger. She turned and called, "Petrus!" A slight, scrawny man came out and stood beside her. In Afrikaans she said, "You don't recognize me. I am Lettie Coetsee – my name was Lettie Badenhorst and this is my husband, Petrus."

Pages of the calendar snapped back to Spitskop School, to slender Lettie Badenhorst with the glossy, black hair who had played the witch in "Snow White" and who was now the mother of nine thin, sun-tanned children who stared at us from their sandpit or from the inside of their house. She invited us inside her home. Half a dozen cheap kitchen chairs were scattered round a chipped formica table. A bed along one wall provided more seating. Through one door we could see what served as a kitchen, and another door revealed two double beds and a cot. These items and an enamel cooking range comprised the only furniture in the house – there were neither carpets, curtains, books nor toys, and everything was dirty and unkempt.

We were offered coffee in tin mugs and the children were each given a drink of water. Within minutes they were all playing outside.

I asked what had become of the old house. Lettie had not moved from the area yet the struggle of trying to bring up a large family amidst such deprivation had left a sad legacy – she seemed to know little about the history of the house she lived in, and to care even less. She and her husband had tried to eke out a living on the farm, but the soil was too thin and drought had set in and like so many in the area, they intended to abandon the farm and make a new life for themselves in Johannesburg, where they were to stay initially with Petrus's sister. We wondered afterwards if any of the children had attended school at all, as Spitskop School had long since been demolished, and the family owned no obvious form of transport.

After a while, our attempts at conversation flagged and we asked Lettie and her husband if we could have a look round the site of our old home again before we headed back to the hotel. We searched all around for the pigsties, the dairy, hen house, storeroom, stable, Old John's hut and the orchard, but there was no trace of them.

I sat down amid the desolation and watched lizards as they scuttled across the stones or lay flat and motionless, basking on the hot concrete. Grasshoppers jumped up and down, clicking loudly in the dry, brittle brown grass while hundreds of beautiful butterflies fluttered and floated noiselessly about in the hot, still air.

I stood on the cornerstone of the house and looked down towards the river which seemed to have changed its course. The veld, too, looked familiar yet somehow different. Only the

193

mountain was unchanged: the baboons still barked and screamed, and the monkeys chattered noisily as they played among the rocks and trees. Further up the mountain, the dassies still made their strange croaking noises and high above, fish eagles wheeled, their cries echoing along the cliff face.

It was impossible to recapture the past and try to connect it to the present. The years had stretched between and the gap was too great. We had been gone too long and during that time the bush had reclaimed what rightfully belonged to it and the mountain was at peace. I had a strange feeling that my presence there now was an intrusion.

We picked our way down towards the road where we had parked the cars, and scratched, torn and bruised, we got in and sat down. We listened for a while to the shrilling of dozens of cicadas, and the repetitive call of the "Piet-my-vrou" bird.

The engines revved into life and we drove away.

CHAPTER 14
THE DANCERS

Some distance further on, we saw a square brick house standing about half a mile off the road. Aubrey and I needed to speak to someone - anyone - who knew what had happened to Dalemain, and as this was likely to be the only dwelling for miles around, we followed the track that led through the gate up to the front door. The cars stopped in a cloud of dust. In front of the house, several dogs of various shapes and sizes, barking and wagging their tails, surrounded us, jumped up at the car and tried to lick us.

A tall, sun-tanned young Afrikaans man came out towards us, sharply called off all the dogs and greeted us with a friendly, "Goeie môre." Aubrey got out of the car and shook hands. The man introduced himself as Jan Venter. He asked when he noticed the Durban registration number whether we had either lost our way or if we needed water or petrol. Aubrey said, "No, thank you, but we've just driven past a place where there once was a farm bordering the Hout River on that pointed mountain west of Mara, just after the Sand River bridge. We see it's in ruins now, with no trace of how it once used to be. Can you give us any information about it because we're very interested to know what has happened to it?"

The man spoke in broken English. "O ja, that place. Yes, I do know, but won't you all first come in out of this sun and have some coffee and beskuit. It's much too hot to stand out here and talk."

We were all very grateful, especially the children who were by now thirsty, irritable and tired of travelling. We climbed out of the cars and followed him into the tin-roofed house. A small wooden table with four chrome and formica chairs in one corner faced a leather three-piece suite at the other end of the room. The children all sat on the cool, red, concrete floor.

He called to his wife, Anna. A shy, very plump young woman came into the room, followed by four young children who clung onto the back of her skirt. Anna could not speak much English, so mostly remained silent excepting when she told the

195

children behind her to "go play in the shade." This they did not seem inclined to do, because they found it much more interesting to peep out at us from behind their mother. If we happened to look at them they darted back into the folds of her skirt.

Anna called to her maid to "Bring coffee and beskuit, please, Maria, and some orange juice for the children." Maria appeared at the kitchen door and counted all the grown-ups with the fingers on one hand and counted the children on the fingers of her other hand. However, this method of calculation was obviously not satisfactory so she first counted the grown-ups, went to count the cups for coffee then came back and counted the children separately.

When she reappeared she carried a large tray of orange juice, strong, home-roasted coffee in cheap, thick cups, and rusks. Anna told Maria to take all the children and the beakers of juice outside to the shade of a wild fig tree. The children looked at each other shyly before they followed Maria outside. Very soon they were laughing, shouting and playing together.

The Venters were naturally curious about us. Jan Venter asked where we had come from and where we were staying, and how we liked the hot weather of the Northern Transvaal. We told him that we had travelled from Durban and were holidaying in Louis Trichardt. His curiosity satisfied, he began to tell us the story of Dalemain.

You know, you are not the first people to come ask me about that place and the family who used to live there thirty years ago. I suppose they come here because my house is the first place they find and because very few people live in this district. There is too much drought and malaria for anyone to make a living in these parts.

The story is that many years ago, a Mr Mathews, an Englishman, his wife and two children, a boy and a girl, lived there. The family lived for a few years in the rondavels but Mr Mathews worked hard and made many improvements to the place. The farm was way up the mountain, and so wild with thick bush growing right up to the doors. A lot of people can't understand why they lived there – but there is a wonderful view from that house. The mountain is just as nature meant it to be, wild and magical – maybe you don't know what I mean and maybe you have to be born in the bushveld to know it like that.

I knew so well what he meant. The mountain had indeed cast its spell on us. He continued:

Soon after they went to live there, Mr Mathews got the farm workers to cut the bush right back. He built a wall round the clearing to keep out the wild animals. I tell you, that mountain was full of snakes and wild animals and they say even leopards used to live up there and you could clearly hear them grunting and growling at night. It was scary.

A few years, maybe about six years later, Mr Mathews decided to build a house just behind the rondavels. He made all his own bricks from clay and sand from the riverbed, and he fired them in a home-made kiln on the farm. I tell you, man, people say that they were good, strong red bricks and that was a well-built house.

When the bricks were all ready, he got some workers to dig the foundations. Then about three feet down they started digging up bones and a bit further down they found some human skulls and skeletons. The men digging the foundations were afraid of what they had found; they all laid down their picks and shovels and went to talk to their boss boy, who was one of their most respected elders. They told him what they had unearthed and said they did not want to dig any further down.

Their boss boy went to Mr Mathews, told him what had happened and begged him to find another site because the men were afraid that a curse would be laid on them and the house. Mr Mathews wouldn't listen and couldn't be persuaded to find another site, and he said it was all just African superstitious nonsense. He said to his boss boy to tell the builders to dig a deep hole behind the stone wall and put all the bones they dug up into the hole, and then get on with the digging again. Man, those builders, they didn't want to do that, not with their ancestors buried there. They asked their boss boy – who was also very unhappy – to go to Mr Mathews and try to get him to change his mind. They warned him that the spirits of the bones would not rest, and only bad luck would come and a curse would be laid on the house and on him. Anyway, Mr Mathews ignored all of that and the digging started again.

Eventually the foundations were laid, the house was built and the big hole with the bones buried behind the stone wall was filled up and covered with earth and stones. It was then forgotten about. The new building was known for miles around as "the Englishman's house" (e'Kiawa Moiesemane) and the family was very popular in the area. For the next few years as long as the rains came, they were very happy and everything went well: the cattle got fat, the crops ripened and their children grew strong and healthy.

197

But then after that, things started to go wrong. First came a terrible drought which lasted about three years, and the river dried up and looked like a sandpit. Ag man, we all suffered very badly during that drought: a lot of wild animals starved and many thousands of people died of malaria.

The next thing that happened was a big swarm of locusts that ate all the withered grass and leaves on the bushes. The cattle suffered badly as a result, but Mr Mathews was lucky because he'd built a windmill which stopped them all dying of thirst.

Then one day after a very severe electrical thunderstorm, a terrible veld fire started at one end of that mountain and quickly spread from one end to the other. Jislaaik! It destroyed every tree, bush and blade of grass as it burned its way across the whole mountain. Some of their cattle were burnt to death, the rest grew thinner and weaker and just when there were only a few left, a poisonous weed sprung up across the river and quickly killed the few remaining animals.

Mr Mathews was a broken man. He had worked so hard to change a wilderness into such a wonderful farm and he had put so much money into it that he couldn't take any more. Not long after this he became ill, then he collapsed and died on the farm. Everybody was very sorry to hear of his death because he was well liked and respected. His wife and two children lived on at the farm for a bit longer, but it really was far too wild and lonely for them and they couldn't make a living there, so they packed up and went back to live in England just before the war. Nobody ever heard of them again, because they were all killed in the Second World War during a bombing raid on London.

A few months after the Mathewses left, another English family took over the place to use it as a weekend shooting lodge for their friends and family. Man, that mountain was full of so many wild animals – in fact, it was a hunter's paradise because Mr Mathews wouldn't allow any shooting on his farm at any time. I believe this new family made it really beautiful. They lined the walls of the living-room with wildebeest heads, leopard skins and kudu skins and man, they even had a lion skin on the floor.

The first weekend they were there, they threw a big party and invited a lot of their friends from Joburg round. We heard it was quite some party! It went on till early the next morning, and after the guests all left for home, the family went to bed. A couple of hours later they woke up to find the whole house engulfed in flames. They couldn't save anything and the parents and their children drove back to the city in just their nightclothes.

198

Soon nothing was left standing – no roof, walls or furniture, and even the foundations were badly cracked and damaged beyond repair. That's how it's been left ever since – there's nothing to show that they were ever there. It's all covered by thick bush; the flowers, the vegetable garden and fruit trees are gone and wild animals and snakes have taken over there. I did hear that a family were living on the ruins there, but we don't know anything about them, except that they came from somewhere in the Banyan area. They won't stay there long – that place doesn't like to be disturbed.

I'm sure nobody would ever want to live there again. People round here say that the spirits of the bones, which were dug up under the foundations of the house, vowed revenge after being disturbed by Mr Mathews when the house was built. Now that the house is destroyed, these spirits dance and sing happily round the ruins when the moon is full and strange noises can be heard echoing from there. These they say are the songs of the spirits singing to their gods. They have got their revenge and are now once again free and at peace. Some people say that the spirits of Mr and Mrs Mathews and the two children come back and join in with the spooks and sing and dance when the moon is full. No-one will go near that place at night. You certainly wouldn't catch me going anywhere near it. It's very eerie. It's a strange, sad place.

Yes indeed, a strange and sad story, but stranger still was that I was talked about as a ghost, dancing on Dalemain ruins in the moonlight!

I wondered whether or not I should say, "Mr Venter, I am one of those children. I've recently returned to South Africa from England and am now living in Natal. I wasn't killed during the war in London, so I'm not a ghost." However Jan Venter had believed this story for so long and had probably told it so often, that it was perhaps kinder not to disillusion him.

It was quite late that night when we finally said goodbye to the Venters. We were sad to leave them because they had been very kind and we knew we would probably not see them again.

We drove back along the stony little road that led to the place where the post box marked the entrance to Dalemain. The moon was riding high, though not quite full. We stopped and looked up towards the ruins. The mountain looked strange. Its silhouette seemed to take on a sinister forbidding expression in the moonlight. Would "they" still be there? I wondered as I strained to listen, but all I could hear was an occasional evening breeze in the thorn-bushes.

Through the silences, I heard my mother reading to us on the verandah. Her voice drifted through the moonlight as she recited one of her favourite poems, "The Listener", then faded into the shadows as we stood there, listeners in a landscape.

* * * * *

We stayed for perhaps a few minutes before we started up the engines and drove slowly away, leaving the mountain and the ruins in peace and solitude, quietly dreaming through the aeons.

We had been intruders in a place that had always belonged only to its ghosts and legends.

CHAPTER 15
EPILOGUE - BY VIVIEN

My mother, Nancy's, narrative, which she wrote between the ages of fifty-eight and eighty-four, ends here, though the story continues.

Many years after she returned to South Africa, my mother learned that both Mr and Mrs Moeschell, who had been so hospitable to them all on their trek through the bushveld, had been interned in a Pretoria jail for the duration of the Second World War and their little store had been closed down. My mother and Aubrey were very sorry to hear this as although the Moeschells were German, they had not been supporters of the Nazi party and had for years lived a quiet, peaceful life on their isolated little farm store.

Mr and Mrs Bell stayed on for a short while after my grandmother, my mother and Aubrey left the Mara district, but as the plague of locusts, the drought and the veld fires had forced so many of their customers to leave the area, the Bells were unable to make a living from their store. Mr Bell died of malaria and Mrs Bell and George packed up, sold the contents of the shop then moved to Naboomspruit, a small, dusty little town about two hundred and eighty miles south of Mara, on the Great North Highway.

In 1962 we visited George Bell in Naboomspruit, where he owned a thriving general dealership that sold everything from vegetables to spare parts for tractors. He was married and a grandfather. Although his father had been from Yorkshire, George in apartheid-driven South Africa, spoke with a strong Afrikaans accent and had become vociferously anti-English. He died in the 1960s in Naboomspruit; his wife survived him for a few years.

On the same holiday we met both Mr Van der Merwe of Spitskop School and Mr Van Wyk of Happy Rest School and their families. Mr Van Wyk made me feel uneasy as I found him to be very authoritarian; strangely enough I found Mr Van der Merwe, who had beaten Aubrey so badly, less intimidating.

Like the farms of so many people in the area, unfortunately, the Behrens' farm experienced drought and Mr Behrens died of malaria. After his death, Mrs Behrens, Lionel and Nora moved away to live with Mrs Behrens' daughter and Lionel and Nora's mother, Isa, near Johannesburg.

Many years later, when my mother was working in a pathology laboratory in Durban, she chatted to a patient who apparently knew the Behrens family. He told my mother that Nora's aunt was staying in the Gordon Hotel, just up the road from us. My mother telephoned this lady who, although not particularly interested in her relations, did tell my mother that it would be better for her not to meet Nora. My mother did, however, manage to establish that Nora had married a man with the same surname, Behrens, and moved to Witbank in the Transvaal. My mother wondered why she should be disappointed in Nora if she were to meet her. Gradually, and somewhat grudgingly, her aunt revealed that Nora had become an alcoholic. My mother telephoned several numbers in Witbank in an effort to contact Nora, but nobody knew of her. Was this her friend, and if so, what had life done to turn a pretty, golden-haired little girl into a sad alcoholic, if indeed this had been her fate? We will never know.

Mrs Chomse, who was widowed some years after moving to Johannesburg, occasionally stayed with Aubrey in Durban. She was by then an old lady, though still attractive and very astute. She was well past her seventieth birthday when she married again, this time a rich Australian sheep farmer whom she called "the Major". She emigrated to Australia where she lived the rest of her years. Her grandson subsequently inherited her considerable fortune.

The Chealeses could not make a living in the Soutpansberg, so packed up and left for Johannesburg. They, like so many other farmers in that area, had simply abandoned their little farm; the house crumbled into the earth. Mr Cheales died of malaria; Mrs Cheales and her two boys remained in Johannesburg, where her younger son, Richard, earned a living as an artist and later as a prominent art critic; eventually Mrs Cheales moved to the South Coast of Natal. We met her a few times in her prefabricated and spooky old house at Doonside on the south coast of Natal: a strange, eccentric but friendly old lady surrounded by her beloved cats.

In the late 1960s, Aubrey became a member of the MOTHS (Members Of the Tin Hats, an ex-servicemen's club in Durban). At a meeting of the MOTHS, he was introduced to another member, none other than Eric Rennie, who had helped my grandfather on the farm at Munnik and had learned how not to saw down branches. Eric and his charming wife, Winnie, were managing an isolated up-country trading store at KwaMbonambi, where we occasionally stayed. Their garden sloped down to a deep, muddy river which was infested with crocodiles. Eric had shot some of these creatures which had ventured near the house, and had even claimed the lives of some of his employees. Eric and Winnie eventually sold the shop and retired to a MOTH house in Durban, where they both died in the late 1970s.

Herbert married late in life and bought a farm in the Northern Transvaal near Potgietersrus where he allowed his children freedom similar to that which my mother and Aubrey had known at Dalemain. With income derived from his security business which employed both Robin and in time, also Aubrey, Herbert bought a second farm in Hillcrest, Natal. Herbert died in 1972 and was buried on his farm in the Transvaal at a ceremony attended only by his immediate family and close friends living nearby. Neither Aubrey nor my mother was invited to the funeral. They added their own obituary after one which mentioned Herbert's wife and family, Molly, Norman and Robin. The children of my grandfather's second marriage, Aubrey and Nancy, had never been fully accepted by the children of his first marriage, even though Robin and Herbert had been very fond of my mother and Herbert often used to call in to my parents' flat at Lyme Hall, Florida Road, during his lunch hour (and sometimes, to sleep off the effects of a good lunch) in Durban.

Molly remained single until, well into middle-age, she married an old family friend and returned to England. My mother stayed with her not long before Molly died, and at long last, after many years of having regarded each other with some rivalry for their father's affections, the two half-sisters learned to understand each other and became friends. Molly was very surprised to learn that my mother had once been afraid of her.

My mother's other half-brother, Norman, who had remained in Kenya, called to see us in Durban late one night, when Hilary and I were asleep. This was the only time he and my mother ever met. Eventually he, his wife and family left Kenya and returned to the English Lake District.

Robin retired and for many years lived happily in Durban. Robin last came to see us in England in August 1985; he spent his last days in a care home in Margate, Natal.

Aubrey continued to work as Compound Manager at Herbert's security business for many years, and after Herbert's death, became a security guard of a large tower block in Durban. Aubrey and his family lived in Durban for many years; eventually they moved to the Transvaal where he died of a stroke in 1997.

Of Old John, Andries, Motorcar, and everyone else

Top left: Charlie, Granma, Helen, Caroline, Vivien.

Top right: Hilary

Left: Nancy and Aubrey. Richmond, North Yorkshire, 1988.

from Dalemain, we heard no more. Their huts had long disappeared and they had probably found work elsewhere.

My mother and father eventually decided to return to Darlington, England, six months before he died of lung cancer in January 1985. My father had been a heavy smoker all his adult life and tobacco had taken its toll on his health.

My mother is now the last link with the past. She has survived several operations and illnesses and, at 84 years of age, takes great delight in reading her memoirs, which transport her to the place where she spent such a happy childhood. She has lived near us for twenty years now and enjoys visits from my husband, Charlie, and me, from my sister, Hilary, and from my two daughters, Caroline and Helen.

The years passed peacefully enough after my parents' return to England. The twentieth century merged into the twenty-first century and in order to keep abreast with technology, we bought a computer. One of my tasks was to find out as much about the past as I could from the internet, and print out pages that contained information that may have been of interest to my mother. I discovered a web site that had a photo of a small 1930s shop that had been restored in the Soutpansberg area, and we wondered if it could have been Bells'. I emailed Marietjie Underhay who owns the converted store and now rents it out as a holiday home called Medike, and she replied that the store was not Bells' store, but that it was in the Sand River Gorge near Waterpoort, about twenty kilometres north east of Dalemain. She had heard her father mention many of the people that my mother knew and emailed us some photographs of herself and her family. Her uncle, Douw Breed, was at school with my mother and Aubrey. Many of the Breed family have remained in the area. Bill Eastwood's grandson, one of Marietjie and Hannes Underhay's friends, had heard of the Mathews family from the mountain but apart from my mother, everybody who knew the Mara area and Spitskop Mountain of eighty years ago has now died. Nothing more was heard of the Coetsee family who squatted on the ruins of Dalemain.

My mother, Charlie and I travelled to the mountain in 1975 but the bush would not let us find the footprint in the rock, the flag, the footpath nor any of the other markers that my mother, uncle and grandparents left on Spitskop. All traces of the buildings had gone, yet the windmill blades still creaked forlornly round in the breeze. We paused for a while, then moved on. Some miles further along, we passed the little wooden cross marking the Voortrekker grave that my mother had seen on her trek through the Soutpansberg.

There is nothing to mark my grandfather's grave in Louis Trichardt cemetery.

* * * * *

In 1992 my mother flew out to South Africa. She and Aubrey, now 70 and 72 years old, drove for the last time to Spitskop. Bush had encroached upon much of the old road and covered over all traces of the people who had once lived there. The windmill had fallen and lay still, one of its blades stuck in the dust; another, pointing to the sun.

The mountain was alone and at rest.

Perhaps the souls who were disturbed when their graves were exhumed to make way for the foundations of the new house had at last made their peace with the Mathews family of Dalemain; perhaps on moonlit nights, they do indeed all join together in dancing on the dust.

The mountain, the bush, the rondavels, with Mabel just visible below and right of the windmill.

---oOo---

For the leading lady of the dance:
Harriet Mabel Mathews.

Nancy Mathews 2006

Vivien Smith 2006